WRITER-FILES

General Editor: Simon Trussler

Associate Editor: Malcolm Page

File on
COWARD

Compiled by Jacqui Russell

Methuen. London and New York

A Methuen Paperback
First published in 1987 as a paperback original
by Methuen London Ltd,
11 New Fetter Lane, London EC4P 4EE
and Methuen Inc, 29 West 35th Street,
New York, NY 10001

Copyright in the compilation
© 1987 by Jacqui Russell
Copyright in the series format
© 1987 by Methuen London Ltd
Copyright in the editorial presentation
© 1987 by Simon Trussler

Typeset in IBM 9pt Press Roman
by ⩔ Tek Art Ltd, Croydon, Surrey
Printed in Great Britain by
Richard Clay (The Chaucer Press) Ltd,
Bungay, Suffolk.

British Library Cataloguing in Publication Data

Russell, Jacqui
    File on Coward. — (Writer-files)
    1. Coward, Noël — Criticism and
    interpretation
    I. Title   II. Series
    822'.912   PR6005.085Z/

ISBN 0-413-53640-8

*Cover image based on a photo by Cecil Beaton.
Thanks are due to Martin Tickner for
his help in the preparation of this volume.*

Contents

The theatre is, by its nature, an ephemeral art: yet it is a daunting task to track down the newspaper reviews, or contemporary statements from the writer or his director, which are often all that remain to help us recreate some sense of what a particular production was like. This series is therefore intended to make readily available a selection of the comments that the critics made about the plays of leading modern dramatists at the time of their production — and to trace, too, the course of each writer's own views about his work and his world.

In addition to combining a uniquely convenient source of such elusive *documentation,* the 'Writer-Files' series also assembles the *information* necessary for readers to pursue further their interest in a particular writer or work. Variations in quantity between one writer's output and another, differences in temperament which make some readier than others to talk about their work, and the variety of critical response, all mean that the presentation and balance of material shifts between one volume and another; but we have tried to arrive at a format for the series which will nevertheless enable users of one volume readily to find their way around any other.

Section 1, 'A Brief Chronology', provides a quick conspective overview of each playwright's life and career. *Section 2* deals with the plays themselves, arranged chronologically in the order of their composition: information on first performances, major revivals, and publication is followed by a brief synopsis (for quick reference set in slightly larger, italic type), then by a representative selection of the critical response, and of the dramatist's own comments on the play and its theme.

Section 3 offers concise guidance to each writer's work in non-dramatic forms, while *Section 4,* 'The Writer on His Work', brings together comments from the playwright himself on more general matters of construction, opinion, and artistic development. Finally, *Section 5* provides a bibliographical guide to other primary and secondary sources of further reading, among which full details will be found of works cited elsewhere under short titles, and of collected editions of the plays — but not of individual titles, particulars of which will be found with the other factual data in Section 2.

The 'Writer-Files' hope by striking this kind of balance between information and a wide range of opinion to offer 'companions' to the study of major playwrights in the modern repertoire — not so as to allow any single line of approach to predominate, but rather to encourage readers to form their own judgements of the plays.

Noël Coward was not only a playwright and lyricist but a distinguished actor and cabaret performer, as well as a skilled director — and an unabashed promoter of his own public image. So it was in part his own fault that the more unsympathetic critics should have scratched naggingly away at that self-polished veneer and failed to recognize the consummate professional beneath. Coward's tendency as a polemicist to blame other writers (and actors) for not following his own recipe for success — notably in his wholesale dismissal of most drama and dramatists after 1956 — also rebounded on him, as the social values which underpinned his writing fell into decline. Like most writers of mannered comedy, he was a member of the social élite he portrayed, and arguably one of its more strident defenders because he was not born into its ranks.

Not the least useful purpose of this volume, however, is to remind us how astutely self-critical Coward could be of his own work, at least in moods of retrospective realism. His output was prolific, and, as he recognized, uneven. But his best plays have now survived the inevitable period of appearing 'dated' by their immediate trappings, to re-emerge as heightened but temperamentally accurate portrayals of a sector of society which liked to laugh at itself within the safe confines of its own theatre. In that respect, Coward was a not unworthy inheritor of the mantle of Congreve: but no less happily do such plays as *Hay Fever, Private Lives,* or *Blithe Spirit* encourage a heartier laughter at extremes of behaviour which nudge us closer to farce — a much underestimated form, especially when its cutting-edge is tempered by that slight social and (often) sexual dissociation which Coward shared no less with Joe Orton than with Oscar Wilde.

The critical response recorded here reflects, then, the way in which Coward's real but circumscribed genius accorded with the changing temper of the times for which he wrote. It is perhaps sad that the prejudices of those times prevented the kind of acute self-knowledge he displayed about his work from being given more 'serious' dramatic expression: but it is not in the least sad that Coward had an alternative and (as he argues here) no less important outlet, in the comedy of social life.

Simon Trussler

1899 16 Dec., Noël Pierce Coward born in Teddington, Middlesex, eldest surviving son of Arthur Coward, piano salesman and Violet (*née* Veitch). A 'brazen, odious little prodigy', his early circumstances were of refined suburban poverty.

1907 First public appearances in school and community concerts.

1908 Family moved to Battersea and took in lodgers.

1911 First professional appearance as Prince Mussel in *The Goldfish*, produced by Lila Field at the Little Th., and revived in same year at Crystal Palace and Royal Court Th. Cannard, the page-boy, in *The Great Name* at the Prince of Wales Th., and William in *Where the Rainbow Ends* with Charles Hawtrey's Company at the Savoy Th.

1912 Directed *The Daisy Chain* and stage-managed *The Prince's Bride* at Savoy in series of matinees featuring the work of the children of the *Rainbow* cast. Mushroom in *An Autumn Idyll*, ballet, Savoy. Appeared with Hawtrey in sketch *A Little Fowl Play*, Coliseum. William in *Where the Rainbow Ends*, now at Garrick.

1913 An angel (Gertrude Lawrence was another) in Basil Dean's production of *Hannele*. Tommy, 'the infant aviator', in *War in the Air*, London Palladium. Understudied part of Buster in Hawtrey's production of *Never Say Die*, Apollo. Slightly in *Peter Pan*, Duke of York's.

1914 Toured in *Peter Pan*. Collaborated with fellow performer Esmé Wynne on songs, sketches, and short stories — 'beastly little whimsies'.

1915 Slightly in *Peter Pan*, Duke of York's. Admitted to sanatorium for tuberculosis. After convalescence played the Slacker in *Where the Rainbow Ends*, Garrick.

1916 Five month tour as Charley in *Charley's Aunt*. Walk-on in *The Best of Luck*, Drury Lane. Wrote first full-length song, 'Forbidden Fruit'. Basil Pycroft in *The Light Blues*, produced by Robert Courtneidge, with daughter Cicely also in cast, Shaftesbury. Short spell as dancer at Elysée Restaurant (subsequently the Café de Paris). Jack Morrison in *The Happy Family*, Prince of Wales Th.

1917 'Boy pushing barrow' in D.W. Griffith's film

Hearts of the World. Leicester Boyd in *Wild Heather,* Gaiety, Manchester. Co-author with Esmé Wynne of one-acter *Ida Collaborates,* Th. Royal, Aldershot. Ripley Guildford in *The Saving Grace,* with Charles Hawtrey, 'who . . . taught me many points of comedy acting', Garrick. Family moved to Pimlico and re-opened boarding house.

1918   Called-up for army. Medical discharge after nine months. Wrote unpublished novels *Cats and Dogs* (loosely based on Shaw's *You Never Can Tell*) and the unfinished *Cherry Pan* ('dealing in a whimsical vein with the adventures of a daughter of Pan'), and lyrics for Darewski and Joel, including 'When You Come Home on Leave' and 'Peter Pan'. Also composed 'Tamarisk Town'. Sold short stories to magazines. Wrote plays *The Rat Trap, The Last Trick* (unproduced) and *The Impossible Wife* (unproduced). Courtenay Borner in *Scandal,* Strand Th.

1919   *Woman and Whisky* (co-author Esmé Wynne) produced at Wimbledon Th. Ralph in *The Knight of the Burning Pestle,* Birmingham Repertory Th., played with 'a stubborn Mayfair distinction' demonstrating a 'total lack of understanding of the play'. Collaborated on *Crissa,* an opera, with Esmé Wynne and Max Darewski (unproduced). Wrote *I'll Leave It to You.*

1920   Bobbie Dermott in *I'll Leave It to You,* New Th. Ralph in *The Knight of the Burning Pestle,* Kingsway. Wrote play *Barriers Down* (unproduced). *I'll Leave It to You* published, London.

1921   On holiday in Alassio, met Gladys Calthrop for the first time. Clay Collins in American farce *Polly with a Past:* during the run 'songs, sketches, and plays were bursting out of me'. Wrote *The Young Idea, Sirocco,* and *The Better Half.* First visit to New York, and sold parts of *A Withered Nosegay* to *Vanity Fair* and short-story adaptation of *I'll Leave It to You* to *Metropolitan.* House-guest of Laurette Taylor and Hartley Manners, whose family rows inspired the Bliss household in *Hay Fever.*

1922   *Bottles and Bones* (sketch) produced in benefit for Newspaper Press Fund, Drury Lane. *The Better Half* produced in 'grand guignol' season, Little Th. Started work on songs and sketches for *London Calling!* Adapted Louise Verneuil's *Pour avoir Adrienne* (unproduced). Wrote *The Queen Was in the Parlour* and *Mild Oats.*

1923   Sholto Brent in *The Young Idea,* Savoy. Juvenile lead in *London Calling!* Wrote *Weatherwise, Fallen Angels,* and *The Vortex.*

1924 Wrote *Hay Fever* (which Marie Tempest at first refused to do, feeling it was 'too light and plotless and generally lacking in action') and *Easy Virtue*. Nicky Lancaster in *The Vortex*, produced at Everyman by Norman MacDermott.

1925 Established as a social and theatrical celebrity. Wrote *On with the Dance*, with London opening in spring followed by *Fallen Angels* and *Hay Fever*. Coward replaced in *The Vortex* by John Gielgud, to free him for American production, Sept. *Hay Fever* and *Easy Virtue* produced, New York. Wrote silent screen titles for Gainsborough Films.

1926 Toured USA in *The Vortex*. Wrote *This Was a Man*, refused a licence by Lord Chamberlain but produced in New York (1926), Berlin (1927), and Paris (1928). *Easy Virtue, The Queen Was in the Parlour*, and *The Rat Trap* produced, London. Played Lewis Dodd in *The Constant Nymph*, directed by Basil Dean, replaced in October by Gielgud to free him to supervize Dean's American production of *This Was a Man*. Wrote *Semi-Monde* and *The Marquise*. Bought Goldenhurst Farm, Kent, as country home. Dec., sailed for Hong Kong on holiday but trip broken in Honolulu by nervous breakdown.

1927 *The Marquise* opened in London while Coward was still in Hawaii, and *The Marquise* and *Fallen Angels* produced, New York. Finished writing *Home Chat*. *Sirocco* revised after discussions with Basil Dean and produced, London.

1928 Clark Storey in Behrman's *The Second Man*, directed by Dean. Gainsborough Films productions of *The Queen Was in the Parlour*, *The Vortex* (starring Ivor Novello), and *Easy Virtue* (directed by Alfred Hitchcock) released – but only the latter, freely adapted, a success. *This Year of Grace* produced, London, and, with Coward directing and in cast, New York. Made first recording, featuring numbers from this show. Wrote *Concerto* for Gainsborough Films, intended for Ivor Novello, but never produced. Started writing *Bitter-Sweet*.

1929 Played in *This Year of Grace* (USA) until spring. Directed *Bitter-Sweet*, London and New York. *Week-End* (*Hay Fever*) produced, Paris. Set off on travelling holiday in Far East.

1930 On travels wrote *Private Lives* (1929) and song 'Mad Dogs and Englishmen', the latter on the road from Hanoi to Saigon. In Singapore joined the Quaints, company of strolling English players, as Stanhope for three performances of *Journey's End*. On voyage home wrote *Post-Mortem*, which was 'similar to my performance as Stanhope: confused, under-rehearsed and hysterical'. Directed and played Elyot Chase in *Private Lives,* London, and Fred in *Some Other Private Lives.* Started writing *Cavalcade* and unfinished novel *Julian Kane. Au Temps des valses (Bitter Sweet)* produced, Paris.

1931 Elyot Chase in New York production of *Private Lives.* Directed *Cavalcade,* London. Film of *Private Lives,* produced by Metro-Goldwyn-Mayer, released in USA (UK, 1932). At end of year set off on trip to South America.

1932 On travels wrote *Design for Living* (on hearing that Alfred Lunt and Lynn Fontanne finally free to work with him) and material for new revue including songs 'Mad about the Boy', 'Children of the Ritz' and 'The Party's Over Now'. As *Words and Music,* with book, music, and lyrics exclusively by Coward and directed by him, produced, London. The short-lived Noël Coward Company, independent company which enjoyed his support, toured UK with *Private Lives, Hay Fever, Fallen Angels,* and *The Vortex.*

1933 Directed *Design for Living,* New York, and played part of Leo. Films of *Cavalcade, To-Night Is Ours* (remake of *The Queen Was in the Parlour*), and *Bitter Sweet* released. Directed London revival of *Hay Fever. Les Amants terribles (Private Lives)* produced, Paris. Wrote *Conversation Piece* as vehicle for Yvonne Printemps, and hit song 'Mrs. Worthington'.

1934 Directed *Conversation Piece* in London and played part of Paul. Cut links with C.B. Cochran and formed own management in partnership with John C. Wilson. Appointed President of the Actors' Orphanage, in which he invested great personal commitment until resignation in 1956. Directed Kaufman and Ferber's *Theatre Royal,* Lyric Th., and Behrman's *Biography,* Globe. Film of *Design for Living* released, London. *Conversation Piece* opened, New York. Started writing *Present Indicative.* Wrote *Point Valaine.*

1935 Directed *Point Valaine,* New York. Played lead in film *The Scoundrel* (Astoria Studios, New York). *Sérénade à trois (Design for Living)* produced, Paris. Wrote *To-Night at 8.30.*

1936 Directed and played in *To-Night at 8.30,* London and New York. Directed *Mademoiselle* by Jacques Deval, Wyndhams. *Les Amants terribles* filmed, Paris.

1937 Played in *To-Night at 8.30,* New York, until second breakdown in health in March. Directed (and subsequently disowned) Gerald Savory's *George and Margaret,* New York.

Wrote *Operette,* with hit song 'The Stately Homes of England'. *Present Indicative* published, London and New York.

1938   Directed *Operette,* London. *Words and Music* revised for American production as *Set to Music.* Appointed adviser to newly-formed Royal Naval Film Corporation.

1939   Directed New York production of *Set to Music.* Visited Soviet Union and Scandinavia. Wrote *Present Laughter* and *This Happy Breed:* rehearsals stopped by declaration of war. Wrote songs and sketches for revue *All Clear,* London. Appointed to head Bureau of Propaganda in Paris to liaise with French Ministry of Information, headed by Jean Giraudoux and André Maurois. This posting prompted speculative attacks in the press, prevented by wartime secrecy from getting a clear statement of the exact nature of his work (in fact unexceptional and routine). Troop concert in Arras with Maurice Chevalier.

1940   Increasingly 'oppressed and irritated by the Paris routine', given leave to visit USA and report on American isolationism and attitudes to war in Europe. Return to Paris prevented by German invasion. Arranged evacuation of children from Actors' Orphanage and returned to USA to do propaganda work for Ministry of Information. Propaganda tour of Australia and New Zealand, and fund-raising for war charities. Wrote play *Time Remembered* (unproduced).

1941   Mounting press attacks in England because of time spent allegedly avoiding danger and discomfort of Home Front. Wrote *Blithe Spirit,* produced in London (with Coward directing) and New York. MGM film of *Bitter-Sweet* (which Coward found 'vulgar' and 'lacking in taste') released, London. Wrote screenplay for *In Which We Serve,* based on the sinking of HMS Kelly. Wrote songs including 'London Pride.' 'Could You Please Oblige Us with a Bren Gun?', and 'Imagine the Duchess's Feelings'.

1942   Produced and co-directed (with David Lean) *In Which We Serve,* and appeared as Captain Kinross (Coward considered the film 'an accurate and sincere tribute to the Royal Navy'). Played in countrywide tour of *Blithe Spirit, Present Laughter,* and *This Happy Breed,* and gave hospital and factory concerts. MGM film of *We Were Dancing* released.

1943   Finished regional tour. Played Garry Essendine in London production of *Present Laughter* and Frank Gibbons in *This Happy Breed.* Produced *This Happy Breed* for Two Cities Films. Wrote 'Don't Let's Be Beastly to the Germans', first sung on BBC Radio (then banned on grounds of lines 'that Goebbels

11

might twist'). Four-month tour of Middle East to entertain troops.

1944   Feb.-Sept., toured South Africa, Burma, India, and Ceylon. Troop concerts in France and 'Stage Door Canteen Concert' in London. Screenplay of *Still Life*, as *Brief Encounter*. *Middle East Diary*, an account of his 1943 tour, published, London and New York — where a reference to 'mournful little boys from Brooklyn' inspired formation of a lobby for the 'Prevention of Noël Coward Re-entering America'.

1945   'Stage Door Canteen Concert', Paris. *Sigh No More*, with the hit song 'Matelot', completed and produced, London. Started work on *Pacific 1860*. Film of *Brief Encounter* released.

1946   Started writing *Peace in Our Time*. Directed *Pacific 1860*, London.

1947   Gary Essendine in London revival of *Present Laughter*. Supervised production of *Peace in Our Time*. *Point Valaine* produced, London. Directed American revival of *To-Night at 8.30*. Wrote *Long Island Sound* (unproduced).

1948   Replaced Graham Payn briefly in American tour of *To-Night at 8.30*, his last stage appearance with Gertrude Lawrence. Wrote screenplay for Gainsborough film of *The Astonished Heart*. Started work on *Future Indefinite*. Max Aramont in *Joyeux chagrins* (French production of *Present Laughter*). Built house at Blue Harbour, Jamaica.

1949   Christian Faber in film of *The Astonished Heart*. Wrote *Ace of Clubs* and *Home and Colonial* (produced as *Island Fling* in USA and *South Sea Bubble* in UK).

1950   Directed *Ace of Clubs*, London. Wrote *Star Quality* (short stories) and *Relative Values*.

1951   Deaths of Ivor Novello and C.B. Cochran. Paintings included in charity exhibition in London. Wrote *Quadrille*. One-night concert at Theatre Royal, Brighton, followed by season at Café de Paris, London, and beginning of new career as leading cabaret entertainer. Directed *Relative Values*, London, which restored his reputation as a playwright after run of post-war flops. *Island Fling* produced, USA.

1952   Charity cabaret with Mary Martin at Café de Paris for Actors' Orphanage. June cabaret season at Café de Paris. Directed *Quadrille*, London. *Red Peppers*, *Fumed Oak*, and *Ways and Means* (from *To-Night at 8.30*) filmed as *Meet Me To-Night*. Sept., death of Gertrude Lawrence: 'no one I have ever known, however brilliant . . . has contributed quite what she contributed to my work'.

1953 Completed *Future Indefinite.* King Magnus in Shaw's *The Apple Cart.* Cabaret at Café de Paris, again 'a triumphant success'. Wrote *After the Ball.*

1954 *After the Ball* produced, UK. Introduced Marlene Dietrich for one night at Café de Paris. July, mother died. Sept., cabaret season at Café de Paris. Nov., Royal Command Performance, London Palladium. Wrote *Nude with Violin.*

1955 June, opened in cabaret for season at Desert Inn, Las Vegas, and enjoyed 'one of the most sensational successes of my career'. Played Hesketh-Baggott in film of *Around the World in Eighty Days,* for which he wrote own dialogue. Oct., directed and appeared with Mary Martin in TV spectacular *Together with Music* for CBS, New York. Revised *South Sea Bubble* (produced as *Island Fling,* USA).

1956 Charles Condomine in television production of *Blithe Spirit,* for CBS, Hollywood. For tax reasons took up Bermuda residency. Resigned from presidency of the Actors' Orphanage. *South Sea Bubble* produced, London. Directed and played part of Frank Gibbons in television production of *This Happy Breed* for CBS, New York. For one night only at Carnegie Hall, conducted New York Philharmonic playing his own music. Co-directed *Nude with Violin* with John Gielgud (Eire and UK), opening to press attacks on Coward's decision to live abroad. Wrote play *Volcano* (unproduced).

1957 Directed and played Sebastian in *Nude with Violin,* New York. *Nude with Violin* published, London.

1958 Played Gary Essendine in *Present Laughter* alternating with *Nude with Violin* on US West Coast tour. Wrote ballet *London Morning* for London Festival Ballet. Wrote *Look after Lulu!*

1959 *Look after Lulu!* produced, New York, and by English Stage Company at Royal Court, London. Film roles of Hawthorne in *Our Man in Havana* and ex-King of Anatolia in *Surprise Package. London Morning* produced by London Festival Ballet. Sold home in Bermuda and took up Swiss residency.

1960 *Waiting in the Wings* produced, Eire and UK. *Pomp and Circumstance* (novel) published, London and New York.

1961 Alec Harvey in television production of *Brief Encounter* for NBC, USA. Directed American production of *Sail Away*. *Waiting in the Wings* published, New York.

1962 Wrote music and lyrics for *The Girl Who Came to Supper* (adaptation of Rattigan's *The Sleeping Prince*, previously filmed as *The Prince and the Showgirl*). *Sail Away* produced, UK.

1963 Guest appearance in film *Paris When It Sizzles*. Visited Australia to supervise production of *Sail Away*. *The Girl Who Came to Supper* produced, USA. Revival of *Private Lives* at Hampstead signals renewal of interest in his work.

1964 'Supervised' production of *High Spirits*, musical adaptation of *Blithe Spirit*, Savoy Th. Introduced Granada TV's 'A Choice of Coward' series, which included *Present Laughter, Blithe Spirit, The Vortex,* and *Design for Living.* Directed *Hay Fever* for National Theatre, first living playwright to direct his own work there.

1965 Played the landlord in film, *Bunny Lake is Missing.* Wrote *Suite in Three Keys.* Badly weakened by attack of amoebic dysentry contracted in Seychelles.

1966 Played in *Suite in Three Keys,* London, which taxed his health further. Started adapting his short story *Star Quality* for the stage.

1967 Caesar in TV musical version of *Androcles and the Lion* (score by Richard Rodgers), New York. Witch of Capri in film *Boom,* adaptation of Tennessee Williams's play *The Milk Train Doesn't Stop Here Any More.* Lorn Loraine, Coward's manager, and friend for many years, died, London. Worked on new volume of autobiography, *Past Conditional.*

1968 Played Mr. Budger, the criminal mastermind, in *The Italian Job.*

1970 Awarded knighthood in New Year's Honours List.

1971 Tony Award, USA, for Distinguished Achievement in the Theatre.

1972 BBC Radio interviews with Edgar Lustgarten.

1973 26 March, died peacefully at his home in Blue Harbour, Jamaica. Buried on Firefly Hill.

The Rat Trap

Play in four acts (reduced to three in production).
Written: 1918.
First London production: Everyman Th., Hampstead,
    18 Oct. 1926 (with Joyce Kennedy as Sheila
    Brandreth, Robert Harris as Keld Maxwell, and
    Raymond Massey as Edmund Crowe).
Published: London: Benn, 1924; in *Three Plays*; and in
    Play Parade, Vol. 3.

*The first act is merely a short sketch to get things going,
with a good deal of the sort of wit in it that Mr. Coward
would probably consider rather poor taste these days.
And the last act does not stand on its own legs, containing as it does a hackneyed infidelity on the part of the
husband, a last-minute baby for the wife (the familiar*
tour de force *that winds up so many of the worst plays
of all languages) and the discovery on the part of the
wife that she is inevitably bound to the husband in consequence. Why? She could have got her divorce equally
well a year later. But the long quarrel and its contentions
remain fine work.*

> Hubert Griffith, *Evening Standard*, 19 Oct. 1926

The Rat Trap I never saw at all as it was produced . . .
while I was away in America. It was written when I was
eighteen, and was my first attempt at serious playwriting.
As such it is not without merit. There is some excruci-
atingly sophisticated dialogue in the first act of which,
at the time, I was inordinately proud. From the point
of view of construction it is not very good except for
the two principal quarrel scenes. The last act is an
inconclusive shambles and is based on the sentimental
assumption that the warring egos of the man and wife
will simmer down into domestic bliss merely because the
wife is about to have a dear little baby. I suppose that I
was sincere about it at the time. . . .

> Coward, 'Preface' to *Play Parade, Vol. 3*

I'll Leave It to You

Light comedy in three acts.
Written: 1919.
First London production: New Th., 21 July 1920 (dir. Stanley
    Bell; with Kate Cutler as Mrs. Dermott, E. Holman Clark as
    Daniel Davis, and Coward as Bobbie).
First American production: Copley Th., Boston 1923.
Revived: 'Q' Theatre, London, 1926.
Published: London: Samuel French, 1920; and in *Play Parade
    Vol. 3.*

*A mysterious but familiar uncle . . . prescribes the work cure for
sleeping sickness when he promises to leave all he has to the
nephew or niece who makes most money. He is not, of course,
going to live long, so that one of them will soon have the great
possessions they take on trust.*

The joke is well sustained and points the moral that if the uncle
had really been rich instead of being almost a pauper, one of the
youngsters would have had no further need to work. . . . Freshly
written and brightly acted, the piece betrays a certain striving
after ultra-comic effect. Mr. Noël Coward, the author, who is not
yet twenty-one, is almost too successful in making the younger
nephew a most objectionable boy. But Miss Kate Cutler is perfect
as the children's absurdly young mother. Inconsequent, tender-
hearted, and altogether charming, she converts a conventional
figure of fun into a vivid, comical character.
Daily Mail, 22 July 1920

Gilbert Miller . . . went on to say that he himself had a good idea
for a light comedy, but that he would like me to write it. Prefer-
ably with Charles Hawtrey in mind, and that if I did it well
enough, he would produce it in London during the following
spring.
    I was then, as I am now, extremely chary of the thought of
writing anything based upon somebody else's idea, but I per-
severed, and within the next few weeks manufactured an amiable
little play. . . . The dialogue, on the whole, was amusing, and
unpretentious, and the construction was not bad, but it was too
mild and unassuming to be able to awake any really resounding

echoes in the hearts of the great public, and although I was naturally entranced with it, Gilbert was not quite as enthusiastic as I had hoped he would be. . . . I had at least had the sense to write a part in the play for myself, in which I should undoubtedly, when the moment came, score an overwhelming personal triumph.

Coward, *Present Indicative,* p. 131-2

The Young Idea

'Comedy of Youth' in three acts.
Written: 1921.
First London production: Savoy Th., 1 Feb. 1923 (dir. Robert Courtneidge; with Herbert Marshall as George Brent, Muriel Pope as Cicely, Ann Trevor as Gerda, and Coward as Sholto).
First American production: Heckscher Th., New York, 17 Mar. 1932.
Published: London; New York: Samuel French, 1924; and in *Play Parade, Vol. 3.*

Sholto and Gerda are both George Brent's children by a wife whom he has allowed to divorce him. They and their mother live in Italy. Brent has now married Cicely, who is continually unfaithful to him and at the moment is 'carrying on' with Rodney Masters. The boy and girl arrive on a visit, sentimentally agog to reunite their father and mother, cynically prepared to foster any scheme whereby this might be accomplished. . . . Brother and sister engineer Cicely's elopement, and return to Italy to complete the reconciliation on their mother's side.

Let me reiterate that throughout the play the young folk did not utter a single word which, in the circumstances, could normally have been uttered. They made dialectical, Puck-ish rings round their elders. . . . To judge by the comfortable laughter round about me, other people seemed to find the play easier of apprehension; perhaps they just took the excellent jokes as they came. But there is something in the make-up of this young playwright beyond the mere *farceur.* . . . I look to him not for 'heart interest' but for the gentle castigation of manners. Let Mr. Coward go on to give us closely observed people babbling of matters of general interest and not, sempiternally, of their green passions.

James Agate, *Saturday Review,* 17 Feb. 1923

17

The Young Idea . . . was primarily inspired by Shaw's *You Never Can Tell.* Dolly and Phillip being my original prototypes for Sholto and Gerda, I felt rather guilty of plagiarism, however inept, and when the play was finished, J.E. Vedrenne kindly sent it to Shaw, to find out whether or not he had any objections. A short while afterwards, I received my script back from Shaw, scribbled all over with alterations and suggestions, and accompanied by a long letter . . . the gist of [which] was that I showed every indication of becoming a good playwright, providing that I never again in my life read another word that he, Shaw, had ever written.

Coward, *Present Indicative*, p. 140

[Shaw's letter, once thought lost, is reprinted in full in Cole Lesley's *The Life of Noël Coward*, p. 65.]

Sirocco

Play in three acts.
Written: 1921 (rewritten 1927).
First London production: Daly's Th., 24 Nov. 1927 (dir. Basil Dean; des. Gladys Calthrop; with Frances Doble as Lucy Griffin and Ivor Novello as Sirio Marson).
Published: London: Secker, 1927; in *Three Plays with a Preface*; and in *Play Parade, Vol. 3.*

A cold and indifferent husband goes for a business trip, refuses to take his wife; enters the mellifluous Italian artist and – fascination. The second act was not much better. It might have been acted to the strains of music, as mimodrama, as a cinema picture. Noise and bustle at a carnival festa on the Riviera – half the text written in Italian; at length a primitive love scene between the artist and the neglected, love-sick, unquenched young wife. More kisses than words. . . . But the miracle happened. . . Just as the third act was the making of The Vortex, so it was the salvation of Sirocco . . . The scene in which the lovers part – he, still lustful, but quite happy to seek fresh fields; she, satiated, crestfallen, horrified, lonesome, unwilling to accept a conventional pardon from her husband – is magnificent . . . As the lover, Mr. Ivor Novello was the Italian troubadour up to date to the life –

romantic, fervent, wayward, irresponsible, and virile too, in the exuberance bred by sunlit skies.

J.T. Grein, *The Sketch*, 7, Dec. 1927

The young artist failing to get up in the morning, his exit down the street grumbling, with a coat over his pyjamas, to fetch the milk, his temperamental dislike of discussing immediately practical things, and his seeking relief in rhetoric and philandering — all this, and more still, the girl's gradual realization that *she* is the only responsible and remotely capable one of the pair — make a scene that has real breadth of feeling and understanding in it ... It was understandable that the gallery should have laughed a good deal during the love scene in the second act ... a love scene that consists of few words and many kisses is almost more than the silliest parts of the house can stand.

'Tom Tit,' *Evening Standard*, 25 Nov. 1927

I wrote *Sirocco* with enthusiasm and conviction. I thought it finely written and well-constructed. I was also proud of the fact that it was completely different in theme, atmosphere, and characterization from anything I had done hitherto. When it had been rehearsed and produced and greeted with howls of derision from both the public and the press I looked at it again and thought it only passably written and poorly constructed with a tenuous second act and a last act that was weak and indecisive. Also, in a fine flush of self-justification, I thought it badly directed by Basil Dean and inadequately acted. ... It took me some time to realize that what was basically wrong was the whole play.

Coward, 'Preface' to *Play Parade*, Vol. 3

[For Basil Dean's account, see his *Seven Stages: an Autobiography*, p. 311–12.]

The Better Half

Comedy in one act.
Written: 1921.
First London production: Little Th., 31 May 1922 (dir. Lewis Casson; des. Francis Bull; with Ian Fleming as the Husband and Auriol Lee as Alice).
Unpublished.

Alice is sick of her husband's everlasting nobility and tries to provoke him to a little human brutality. The moment she succeeds she calls him a bully. At last, leaving her husband with a woman as aspiring as himself, she departs in search of a less noble mate.

Clarion, 2 June 1922

The Better Half . . . was wittily played by Auriol Lee. In spite of this it was received with apathy; I think, possibly because it was a satire and too flippant in atmosphere after the full-blooded horrors that had gone before it. Nevertheless, it was quite well written and served the purpose, if only for a little, of keeping my name before the public.

Coward, *Present Indicative,* p. 193

The Queen Was in the Parlour

Romance in three acts.
Written: 1922.
First London production: St. Martin's Th., 24 Aug. 1926; trans. to Duke of York's Th., 4 Oct. 1926 (dir. Basil Dean; with Madge Titheradge as Nadya, Herbert Marshall as Prince Keri, and Francis Lister as Sabien Pastal.)
First American production: Curran Th., San Francisco, 7 Oct. 1929.
Film versions: silent, by Gainsborough Films, 1928 (dir. and adapt. Graham Cutts); remade by Paramount 1933, as *Tonight Is Ours* (dir. Stuart Walker; adapt. Edwin Justus Mayer).
Published: London: Benn, 1926 *(Contemporary British Dramatists* series, No. 50); and in *Play Parade, Vol. 3.*

Today [Sabien] is to be married to Nadya, and is as happy as can be. Leaning from the balcony of her flat, he watches the dawn rise over Paris. And of what does he think? Of her beauty? Of how glad he is that she has laid aside her royalty in the State of Kraja and become an approachable cosmopolitan? Of the coffee that she is brewing, and the cigarettes that will accompany it? Yes, perhaps he thinks of all these things, but, what he talks about is suicide. Not for long, indeed, and not too seriously, but . . . enough to warn the timid that there may be pistols before the end. On the track of the pistol we are conveyed from Paris to Kraja. . . . Here is Nadya become Queen of a country that abounds in pistols and is very doubtfully worth the sacrifice of so amusing a husband as Sabien. That, however, is Nadya's business, and Miss Titheradge, crowned, betrothed to Prince Keri, and on the eve of revolution, makes a tragedy of it with regal dignity and womanly tears. And then just when Prince Keri, who is made gravely and charmingly formal by Mr. Herbert Marshall, is seeming less forbidding than Nadya has feared, just when she thinks she may be able to live for her country, though Sabien languishes in Paris, Sabien turns up again. To-morrow she is to be married; to-night — ? Well, well, she struggles against it. They tremble in their terrible emotion like tissue paper in a draught. But she yields. To-night by a secret staircase, he shall climb to a champagne supper. In the morning, an altar for her and a pistol for him. Then, of course, there is the revolution. It happens most inconveniently. Poor Zana, the confidential maid, is at her wits' end with Prince Keri and General Krish waiting for disaster outside her bedroom door. The Queen has to be disturbed, and while, from the balcony, she is polishing off the mob, we are to imagine Sabien examining his pistol and awaiting the romantic moment. When the moment comes, General Krish is full of tact, and the Prince of understanding. He, too, had loved in vain. So everyone, including the deceased, is content, though so agile a young man as Mr. Lister showed us in Sabien might have been expected to conduct his death with less noise and more discretion.

The Times, 25 Aug. 1926

The Queen was in the Parlour will be old-fashioned long before *The Prisoner of Zenda* and *Rupert of Hentzau*. However, on the whole, I didn't make a bad job of it. The first act in Paris is a little forced and over-hectic but the second and third acts contain some good moments, notably the scene between Keri and Nadya and the characterizations of the Queen Mother and the English governess. General Krish is of course a cliché from the top of his grizzled head to his jingling spurs, but the other characters are redeemed by occasional flashes of originality and, taking into consideration the intrinsic 'Ruritanianism' of the situation, behave reasonably and sensibly.

Coward, 'Preface' to *Play Parade, Vol 3*

Mild Oats

Play in one act.
Written: 1922:
Unperformed.
Published: in *Collected Sketches and Lyrics.*

A young woman pretending to be a 'good time girl' allows herself to be taken to a young man's flat late one night. Finally she breaks down and confesses her respectability.

London Calling!

Revue.
Written: 1922-23, in collaboration with Ronald Jeans.
First London production: by André Charlot, Duke of York's Th., 4 Sept. 1923 (book by Ronald Jeans and Coward; lyrics and music by Coward; with Coward, Gertrude Lawrence, Maisie Gay, and Eileen Molyneux); *revised versions,* with cast changes and new material, 1 Dec. 1923, 20 Feb. 1924.
Published: selections in *The Lyrics of Noël Coward, Collected Sketches and Lyrics,* and *The Noël Coward Song Book.*

There is no reason to despise revue, which springs as much out of the temper of modern minds as Greek drama from Greek thought, or the morality plays from a desire to be preached to. Revue fits the times, and there is no critical sense in being sniffy about this particular form of dramatic art. To begin with, it fulfils its function, which is that of slating public vanities and foibles by laughing at them.

James Agate, *Sunday Times*, 9 Sept. 1923

The hits of the show were primarily Maisie's singing of 'What Love Means to Girls Like Me', and her performance of Hernia Whittlebot, my little burlesque on the Sitwells. [See p. 89 below.] Next in order of applause came Gertie singing 'Carrie', and the duet, 'You Were Meant for Me', which she and I did together, with a dance arranged by Fred Astaire. . . .

The only complete and glorious failure of the whole show was my performance of a single number, 'Sentiment', which had gone so well at the dress-rehearsal and had been so enthusiastically applauded by the friendly company in the stalls that I bounded on at the opening performance fully confident that I was going to bring the house down. . . . I was immaculately dressed in tails, with a silk hat and a cane. I sang every witty couplet with perfect diction and a wealth of implication which sent them winging out into the dark auditorium, where they fell wetly, like pennies into mud. After this, discouraged but not quite despairing, I executed an intricate dance, painstakingly sweated over by Fred Astaire, tapping, after-beating, whacking my cane on the stage, and finally exiting to a spatter of applause led, I suspected, by Mother and Gladys. . . .

During the first two weeks of the run, I received, to my intense surprise, a cross letter from Osbert Sitwell; in fact, so angry was it, that I first of all imagined it to be a joke. However, it was far from being a joke, and shortly afterwards another letter arrived, even crosser than the first. To this day I am still a little puzzled as to why that light-hearted burlesque should have aroused him, his brother, and sister to such paroxysms of fury. But the fact remains that it did, and I believe still does.

Coward, *Present Indicative*, p. 196-7

Weatherwise

Comedy in two scenes.
Written: 1923.
First production: by Noël Coward Company, with *Home Chat*, Festival Th., Malvern, 8 Sept. 1932.
Published: in *Collected Sketches and Lyrics*.

After falling into a trance during a seance, Lady Warple subsequently behaves like a dog at every mention of the weather. Attempts to cure her culminate in her springing at the throat of her psychiatrist and killing him.

Fallen Angels

Comedy in three acts.
Written: 1923.

First London production: Globe Th., 21 Apr. 1925 (dir.
Stanley Bell; with Tallulah Bankhead as Julia Steroll and Edna
Best as Jane Banbury).
First New York production: 49th Street Th., 12 Jan. 1927.
Revived: Ambassadors Th. London, 29 Nov. 1949 (dir. Willard
Stoker; with Hermione Baddeley as Julia Steroll and Hermione
Gingold as Jane Banbury); Vaudeville Th., 4 Apr. 1967.
Published: London: Benn, 1924 (*Contemporary British Dramatists*
Series, No. 25); in *Three Plays;* in *Play Parade, Vol. 2;* and in
Plays: One.

*Julia and Jane are two very, very modern young women [who]
have one unique link in their friendship. Each has had a serious
temporary affair with a conquering French gentleman. . . . Each
has married meanwhile one of those immense, pleasant, un-
reflective golfers. . . . They are happy . . . but they are no longer
in love. . . . Julia has waked that morning with a presentiment.
. . . Jane bursts in. . . . Maurice is coming to London. . . . Two
overwrought young women sit down to a dinner preceded by a
particularly potent cocktail; to peck at excellent food and to split
with unwise enthusiasm a large bottle of champagne followed by
a generous liqueur. . . . Jane . . . falters out of her friend's house
. . . spends the night in an hotel in Bayswater . . . and arrives next
morning in evening dress to find a tangle of trouble. The infuriated
Julia has betrayed her to the disturbed golfer, William. . . . A bell.
The bland and debonair Maurice is announced. . . . His un-
conquerable politeness effectively stymies the hardly-convinced
husbands. Will they all come up and help him chose his curtains?
He has taken the flat just above. The men . . . will not. The two
angels will. . . . .*

An unpleasant subject, you may say? Well, not edifying or
elevating, certainly, but Mr. Noël Coward has written so gaily and
wittily and they play it so lightly and briskly that it is relieved of
all offensiveness. Many a play that draws carefully to a sunny and
happy ending can be and has been furtively offensive all through.
I don't remember a better piece of stage-craft in this type of play
since Mr. Maugham's *Home and Beauty.* . . .

This was emphatically a play for the two women. . . . The
men are mere foils. Even Maurice, who dominates the situation, is

withheld till the last few moments by a very judicious artistry. . . .
Joseph Thorp, *Punch*, 29 Apr. 1925

Fallen Angels has not the merit of a risqué story. It is too en-
nervating, too stuffy, too mailicious. Brilliant in execution, brilliant
in dialogue, and brilliantly acted, it is still nothing more than a
clever play. . . . False to character, false to life — it is false to art.
The cynical conclusion, though devastatingly clever as a curtain
leaves an nasty aftertaste.

The Sketch, 6 May 1925

When *Fallen Angels* was first produced at the Globe Theatre,
London, in the Spring of 1925 it was described by a large section
of the press as amoral, disgusting, vulgar, and an insult to British
womanhood. It was of course none of these things. They might
have said it was extremely slight and needed a stronger last act;
they might, with equal truth and more kindness, have said that it
had an amusing situation, some very funny lines, two excellent
parts for two good actresses, and was vastly entertaining to the
public. . . . I cannot honestly regard it as one of my best comedies
but it is gay and light-hearted and British womanhood has been
cheerfully insulted by it on various occasions for almost a quarter
of a century.

Coward, 'Preface' to *Play Parade, Vol. 2*, revised ed., p. 19

The women can hardly have grace, but they should have a kind of
bubbling juvenile jollity which, remember, was what Edna Best
and Tallulah Bankhead gave it 24 years ago. I have the greatest
respect for our two queens of revue, Hermione Baddeley and
Hermione Gingold: but they are not juvenile bubblers and their
handling of the comedy has the mature vigour of experienced
comediennes. On those lines much of it is wildly funny . . . . It is
the fifties laughing uproariously at what the twenties thought
daring and faintly disquieting. Miss Gingold and Miss Baddeley
are faithful to the text, but that seems to make the burlesque all
the funnier . . . all the play's original weaknesses now become
virtues.

Anthony Cookman, *The Tatler*, 8 Jan. 1950

I have never in my long experience seen a more vulgar, silly, unfunny, disgraceful performance. [Coward, commenting on the try-out, *Diaries*, 23 Nov. 1949.] *Fallen Angels* a terrific success. Livid.

Coward, *Diaries*, 19 Dec. 1949

The Vortex

Play in three acts.
Written: 1923-24.
First London production: Everyman Th., Hampstead, 25 Nov. 1924; trans. to Royalty Th., 16 Dec. 1924; to Comedy Th., 9 Mar. 1925; to Little Th., 4 May 1925 ('rehearsed by the author under the direction of Norman MacDermott'; des. Gladys Calthrop; with Coward as Nicky Lancaster, Lilian Braithwaite as Florence Lancaster, and Mary Robson as Helen Saville).
First New York production: Henry Miller's Th., 16 Sept. 1925.
Revived: Lyric Th., Hammersmith, 4 Mar. 1952; trans. to Criterion Th., 9 Apr. 1952.
Film version: Gainsborough Pictures, 1927 (adapt. and dir. Adrian Brunel).
Published: London: Benn, 1925 *(Contemporary British Dramatists* series, No. 19); in *Three Plays;* in *Play Parade. Vol. 1;* and in *Plays: One.*

The milieu is that of Our Betters, *without the Americans. Into this vicious silly and crazily-perverted minority . . . comes one Nicky Lancaster, who has been finishing his schooling in Paris. He finds his mother languishing on the breast of Tom Veryan, a sturdy young Guards officer – a 'tame cat'. . . . Nicky is himself tarred with the degenerate brush. He dopes, his tongue takes the convenient path of the superlative. . . . But Nicky . . . is in love with a comparatively 'nice' girl, one Bunty Mainwaring . . . a frank little savage, who likes to be amoral, but does not believe in giving vice a halo. And now it appears that Bunty and Veryan are . . . not strangers to one another. . . . Nicky is by way of being a pianist, and he covers up his mother's outburst of jealousy with a crescendo of discordant jazz. . . .*

The third act is a very fine piece of work. . . . [Nicky] tells his mother how he has watched her jig, amble, and lisp, and forces her to a confession. But he is no severe judge, and would understand wantonness. Has his mother a case? She has, but it is a wretched one, and the boy tears it to pieces. . . . He loves her, and if she be but the least bit desirous to be blessed he'll blessing beg of her. And as he lays his sobbing head upon his mother's knees the curtain comes down.

James Agate, *Sunday Times,* 7 Dec. 1924

Practically all of my notices for this play were generously adulatory, though most of them were concerned that I should choose such an 'unpleasant' subject and such 'decadent' types. I have come to the conclusion than an 'unpleasant' subject is something that everybody knows about, but shrinks from the belief that other people know about it too. . . . The minor characters in *The Vortex* drink cocktails, employ superlatives, and sometimes turn on the gramophone. . . . Florence takes lovers occasionally and Nicky takes drugs very occasionally . . . . I consider neither of these vices any more unpleasant than murder or seduction, both of which have been a standing tradition in the English theatre for many years.

Coward, 'Introduction' to *Three Plays*

He does everything wrong on the stage which it is possible to do. He stands in the wrong place, opens a door with the wrong hand, puts the wrong emphasis on his lines, makes, often enough, the wrong faces. And he gets away with it, simply through the immense nervous force which is surging through him. I shall never forget Seymour Hicks . . . standing in his stall cheering the young actor whose manifold faults he had been mercilessly condemning. Noël had done everything wrong with almost tiresome consistency. And the result had been more moving than the most polished performance even of Hicks himself.

The Sketch, March 1927

It may be laboriously stagey in contrivance, and what were once arresting effects — like the frantic piano-playing at every crisis in this neurotic household — may have faded with the years into rather tiresome tricks. But the wit still sparkles and that final hysterical scene between the son and the mother with a lover of just his own age has lost little of its old dramatic sting. Isobel Jeans runs the whole range of the mother's emotions from

desperate kittenishness to a crumpled realization of her age.
Daily Mail, 10 April 1952

Hay Fever

Light comedy in three acts.
Written: 1924.
First London production: Ambassadors Th., 8 June 1925; trans.
Criterion Th., 7 Sept. 1925 (dir. Coward; des. Gladys Calthrop;
with Marie Tempest as Judith Bliss).
First New York production: Maxine Elliott Th., 5 Oct. 1925.
Revived: Shaftesbury Th., 17 Nov. 1933; National Th., 27 Oct.
1964; Queen's Th., 26 Oct. 1983.
Published: London: Benn, 1925 *(Contemporary British Dramatists*
series, No. 27); New York: Harper, 1925; London, New York:
Samuel French, 1927: in *Bitter-Sweet and Other Plays,* In *Play
Parade, Vol 1;* in *My Best Play* (London: Faber, 1934), in
Modern Plays (London: Dent, 1937); and in *Plays: One.*

*The Bliss family – consisting of an ex-actress mother, a novelist
father, and a precocious boy and girl – invite four guests for the
week-end. The visit begins with a tea-party where the family get
fed and the guests left out, and continues with some elaborate
philandering. In the morning the guests steal away quietly while
the family are quarrelling at breakfast. The hostess merely
remarks 'How rude' and the curtain falls.*
The Sketch, 24 June 1925

There is neither health nor cleanness about any of Mr. Coward's
characters, who are still the same vicious babies sprawling upon the
floor of their unwholesome creche. . . . But it would be foolish to
insist upon attacking this play on the score of truth or morality. . . .
As a piece of brilliant, impudent, and sustained fooling the play is
very pleasant entertainment, and well enough 'made' to delight a
Frenchman. The ex-actress who cannot have an emotion without
merging it in one of her old parts or the more dithryambic passages
of her husband's vile novels, the quartet of week-end visitors who
flirt with anybody except the person they were invited down to
the country cottage to flirt with – all this is excellent.
    And then there is the dialogue. . . . This is clean indeed, in the

sense that it is whittled and pared to an admirable fineness. . . . I venture to suggest that many moral plays are not enlivened with such delicate imbecility. . . .

Such plays are bad for the theatre. They appeal to an infinitesimally small and, I believe, purely metropolitan audience. Their success is one almost entirely of curiosity, even of a more of less prurient itch from which the country as a whole is free. . . . Will not Mr. Coward see to it in the future that he has something to say to the country as well as the town?

James Agate, *Sunday Times*, 8 June 1925

The idea came to me suddenly in the garden, and I finished it in about three days. . . . However, when I had finished it . . . I read it through and was rather unimpressed with it. . . . I knew certain scenes were good, especially the breakfast scene in the last act, and the dialogue between the giggling flapper and the diplomat in the first act, but apart from these it seemed to me a little tedious. I think the reason for this was that I was passing through a transition stage as a writer; my dialogue was becoming more natural and less elaborate, and I was beginning to concentrate more on the comedy values of the situation rather than the comedy values of actual lines. I expect that when I read through *Hay Fever* that first time, I was subconsciously bemoaning its lack of snappy epigrams. At any rate, I thought well enough of it to consider it a good vehicle for Marie Tempest. . . .

Coward, *Present Indicative*, p. 208

The degree of distortion is as consistent and the nonsense as purely nonsensical as in *The Importance of Being Earnest*, Wilde's play being superior to Coward's chiefly in its being sprung from a richer fable and in its more elaborate verbal pattern. But the proof that *Hay Fever* is in the same class . . . and has the same rare freedom from emotional alloy lies in the discovery that it does not date. If it had pointed an arrow at contemporary manners, it would already have lost its aim: if love or hope or sadness or hatred or ambition had, even for a moment, intruded upon its fooling, there would be parts of it already tarnished as poor Lady Windermere is, but it is, in the highest mood of fantastic comedy, deliciously heartless and, therefore, deliciously alive and fresh.'

The Times, 13 Nov. 1933

29

Hay Fever is by far and away one of the most difficult plays to perform that I have encountered. To begin with, it has no plot at all, and remarkably little action. Its general effectiveness therefore depends upon expert technique from each and every member of the cast.

Coward, 'Introduction' to *Play Parade, Vol. 1*

The interesting thing about *Hay Fever*, after nearly forty years, is the way in which its two groups of characters have responded to time — the Bliss family in their never-never land remaining untouched by it, and their guests stiffening into period caricatures. The production dwells pointedly on this contrast, weighing down the outsiders with cricket-blazers, and waxed moustaches, and leaving their hosts in dress that spans both periods. The use of costume is one of the many delights of the production, particularly in the second act where . . . it intensifies the agonies of social embarrassment.

The Times, 28 Oct. 1964

Maggie Smith . . . as the *femme fatale* whose femininity grows less fatal as the week-end wears on . . . regards her ill-mannered hosts with a deadpan balefulness, but her right hand is the giveaway and it wields her cigarette-holder and handbag like a rapier and a mace, respectively. . . . I like too Robert Lang's diplomat, game for anything and wandering to and fro, body inclined gently forward as if in anticipation of something nice just around the next corner. Lynn Redgrave's flapper lacked technique but was just right from an instinctive point of view. Miss Redgrave's desperate bid to snatch a tea-cake by stealth was for me one of the highlights of the evening. . . .

Dame Edith was miscast; when she addressed another charater it was in the tones of Catherine the Great calling for Ptomkin; while everyone else was making a soufflé, Dame Edith was cooking a cabbage. . . . Mr. Coward has the distinction of having created an entire era which possibly never existed, but it has the more fascination for that reason.

Hugh Leonard, *Plays and Players,* Dec. 1964

[See also Coward's *Diaries*, April 1964-June 1965.]

Easy Virtue

Play in three acts.
Written: 1924.
First London production: Duke of York's Th., 9 June 1926 (dir. Basil Dean; des. George W. Harris; with Jane Cowl as Larita and Mabel Terry-Lewis as Mrs. Whittaker).
First New York production: Empire Th., 7 Dec. 1925.
Film version: silent, by Gainsborough Pictures, 1927 (adapt. Eliot Stannard; dir. Alfred Hitchcock).
Published: London: Benn, 1926 *(Contemporary British Dramatists* series, No. 26): New York: Harper, 1926; in *Play Parade; Vol. 2;* in *Bitter Sweet and Other Plays;* in *Curtain Calls;* and in *Plays: One.*

The son of a stuffy English country family brings back his 'unsuitable' bride, who, after enduring attempted humiliations notably at the hands of her sisters-in-law, finally puts them to rout.

The piece excited even to the point of making us believe that by taking her hook for Paris . . . Larita showed herself a more admirable creature than the average young Englishwoman who on a wet day puts on thick boots and a mackintosh and tramps the country lanes. It was not till we got home that we reflected that a light and wandering lady is, God help us, a thing of naught. . . .

There are no moments, apparently, in which Mr. Coward, the playwright, refrains from thinking in terms of sex, and to attribute Marion's proselytism to repressed desire seems to me to be just nonsense. Larita's taunts about concealed pruriency should be deleted, the implication being that they are true and not charges made by a woman in a temper.

James Agate, *Sunday Times*, 13 June 1926

Mr. Coward does not tell a story well. He has extraordinary skill in devising theatrical situations, and the end of the second act caused an outburst of enthusiasm from the audience such as I have seldom heard. It is, of course, a familiar device, and one which, when capably done, never fails to excite playgoers. The leading character steadily works up to a climax, and then suddenly goes all out, and down comes the curtain with a rush. Mr. Coward contrived this scene with very great ability. . . . He knows his job and can write dramatic dialogue. This is none of your literary stuff. . . . But I am astonished at the poverty of the first and third act of this play when I can remember the richness of the second. The singular fact about Mr. Coward is that he begins badly and ends badly, but that his middle acts are always excellent. . . . There is no story whatever in the first act. The characters merely assemble.

The Observer, 13 June 1926

Women with pasts to-day receive far more enthusiastic social recognition than women without pasts. The narrow-mindedness, the moral righteousness, and the over-rigid social codes have disappeared but with them has gone much that was graceful, well-behaved, and endearing. It was in a mood of nostalgic regret at the decline of such conventions that I wrote *Easy Virtue*. When it was produced several critics pounced triumphantly on the fact that the play was similar in form and tone and plot to the plays of Pinero. I myself was unimpressed by their perception, for the form and tone and plot of a Pinero play was exactly what I had tried to achieve.

Coward, 'Preface' to *Play Parade*, *Vol. 2*

My object in writing had been primarily to adapt a story, intrinsically Pinero in theme and structure, to present-day behaviour: to compare the *déclassé* woman of to-day with the more flamboyant *demi-mondaine* of the nineties. The line that was intended to establish the play on a basis of comedy rather than tragedy, comes at the end of the second act when Larita, the heroine, irritated beyond endurance by the smug attitude of her 'in-laws', argues them out of the room and collapses on to the sofa where, suddenly catching sight of a statuette of the Venus de Milo on a pedestal, she shies a book at it and says: 'I always hated that damned thing!'

Jane invariably delivered this line in a voice strangled with sobs and brought the curtain down to tremendous applause. If, however, she had said it and played the scene leading up to it with less emotion and more exasperation, I don't think that the play would have received quite so much criticism on the score of being old-fashioned. On the other hand there would probably not have been so much applause.

Coward, *Present Indicative*, p. 268-9

On with the Dance

Revue.
Written: 1924-25.
First London production: by C.B. Cochran, London Pavilion, 30
    Apr. 1925 (book and lyrics by Coward; music by Philip
    Braham and Coward; with Douglas Byng, Nigel Bruce,
    Hermione Baddeley, and Alice Delysia).
Published: selections in *The Lyrics of Noël Coward* and *Collected
    Sketches and Lyrics;* and in *The Noël Coward Song Book.*

The speed of the change from scene to scene, of the performance
of each number, is feverish. . . . M. Massine, who produced the
two amazing ballets, 'The Rake' suggested by the engravings of
Hogarth, and 'Crescendo', an attempt to 'shatter the gentle
tranquillity of *Less Sylphides* by the insistent clamour of
modernity' — both left one gasping — danced brilliantly. . . . But
all, of course, bizarre, preposterous, in so much that the beautiful
stately 'Hungarian Wedding' with which the revue ended almost
perished because the contrast was too great. . . .

One was astonished to find oneself laughing at the sight of
Mr. Ernest Thesiger and Mr. Douglas Byng, dressed as middle-aged
women, disrobing in a bedroom. Or that fragment in the railway
compartment, wherein Mlle. Alice Delysia obtains from Mr.
Nigel Bruce the wherewithal to purchase a sleeper!

After such fare, the whirlwind dancing . . . the extraordinarily
clever skits on old London music-halls, and the drolleries of Miss
Hermione Baddeley, were as welcome as they were remarkable.
          Morning Post, 1 May 1925

The ideas came swiftly and, oddly enough, nearly every idea
carried with it its accompanying song. In my planning of the
show almost every scene led up to a number, and so when the
revue was complete is was discovered, to the embarrassment of
everyone but me, that with the exception of three numbers by
Philip Braham for which I had written the lyrics, a few odd pieces
of classical music for use in ballets, etc., and one interpolated
song for Delysia, the whole score, book and lyrics were mine.
          Coward, *Present Indicative*, p. 241-2

This Was a Man

Comedy in three acts.
Written: 1926.
First New York production: Klaw Th., 23 Nov. 1926 (dir. Basil
  Dean; des. George W. Harris and Gladys Calthrop; with
  Francine Larrimore as Carol Churt, A.E. Matthews as Edward
  Churt, Nigel Bruce as Evelyn Bathurst, and Auriol Lee as Zoe
  St. Mervin). Banned by Lord Chamberlain in UK.
First European production: as *Die Ehe von Welt*, by Max
  Reinhardt at Die Komödie, Berlin, 25 Nov. 1927.
First European production in English: by the English Players at
  Théâtre Albert, Paris, 11 Jan. 1928.
Published: London: Secker; New York: Harper, 1926; in *Three
  Plays with a Preface:* and in *Curtain Calls.*

---

*An impulsive little wretch, Carol Churt, carries on boldly with
almost anyone save her husband. Quite aware of these scandalous
proceedings, Edward Churt, the famous portrait painter, is too
bored to defend his tedious respectability. His closest friend,
however, Major Evelyn Bathurst... proceeds to give Carol a much-
needed lesson. Alone with her in his flat, he leads her to think that
he is enamoured, and then suddenly berates her for her loose
morals. More pliable than he is, she tricks him into betraying her
husband's confidence. Being ostentatiously a man of honour, he
confesses to Edward Churt, who, in a jaded voice, delivers an
emotional ultimatum.*

Mr. Coward's tendency to express his drama in prolonged
conversation between two characters has been carried to an
extreme.... Occasionally the people speak brightly.... For the
most part, however, the talk runs on without distinction, and in
the easiest possible method of playwriting. Whenever a new
character comes on the stage, making the number of those present
actually three, one of them rushes away in high fettle lest the
duologues be interrupted. For characters left stranded, with no one
to talk to at all, there is always the telephone. Common as these
devices may be, they are not unserviceable. But Mr. Coward's insis-
tence on them becomes an exhibition of weakness .... The tone
of *This Was a Man* is obviously serious. But the drama is trifling.

Brooks Atkinson, *New York Times*, 24 Nov. 1926

Many first nighters complained that the dinner scene in the second act was the longest meal they had ever sat through. The play failed in spite of some patches of expert writing, but these alas were not enough to relieve the general tedium. It was not at that time produced in England because the Lord Chamberlain took exception to the fact that when, in the last act, the husband learns that his wife, who is unscrupulous, has seduced his best friend, who is unintelligent, he goes off into gales of laughter. . . . . The fundamental error in the play is the second act which is a long-drawn-out duologue between the wife and the ultimately seduced friend, both of whom are tiresome characters. If he had been written with less meticulous veracity and more wit it might have succeeded but even so I doubt it. Bores on the stage however ironically treated inevitably bore the audience.

Coward, 'Preface' to *Play Parade, Vol. 3*

[See also *The Life of Noël Coward*, p. 115-17.]

The Marquise

'A new comedy.'
Written: 1926.
First London production: Criterion Th., 16 Feb. 1927 (dir.
W. Graham Browne; des. William Nicholson; with Marie
Tempest as the Marquise, Frank Cellier as Estaban, and
W. Graham Browne as the Comte).
First New York production: Biltmore Th., 14 Nov. 1927.
Published: London: Benn, 1927 *(Contemporary British Dramatists*
series, No. 53); in *Play Parade, Vol. 3;* and in *Plays: Two.*

The Comte Raoul de Viraac . . . a reformed sinner, is about to marry his daughter to Miguel, the son of his former boon companion, El Duco de Santaguano . . . but Adrienne adores Jacques Rijar, her father's secretary, while Miguel has lost his heart to a dancer in Paris. A feast is held to celebrate the betrothal, after which the guests depart. Them . . . the Marquise . . . enters. She is the former mistress of the Comte and the mother of Adrienne. . . . The Marquise has come to see her child, and by a pretty trick contrives to be invited to spend the night in the Château de Vriaac. . . . On the following day, El Duco de Santaguano calls and discovers in the Marquise his former mistress and the mother of Miguel!

Thereafter, there are stratagems by which Rijar is married by a terrorized priest to Adrienne, and Comte Raoul, after a duel with El Duco, consents to be married to the Marquise.

Morning Post, 17 Feb. 1927

Once the Marquise is fairly established at the *château* revolution is certain. Observe with what anticipation of triumph she drinks, in her morning chocolate, a toast to the departed Madame de Vriaac; or how, when she encounters Estaban and hears of his son Miguel . . . she laughs away the thought of the absurd betrothal; and see, finally, how she sends for her leather travelling case, how she locks the doors, and how, with no softer persuasion than a brace of pistols, she drives Father Clement into marrying Jacques and Adrienne. Up to that point it is the merriest of games, and Miss Tempest plays it with exquisite gaiety, but with the pistols Mr. Coward's inventiveness exhausts itself. Who cares for the reconciliation between Eloise and Raoul, or for the duel he fights with his old friend? The lovers are away, Father Clement is defeated, all the good secrets are out . . . and Miss Tempest herself cannot save the last act.

The Times, 17 Feb. 1927

I wrote *The Marquise* . . . .with Marie Tempest speaking every line of it in my mind's ear . . . [and on stage] . . . there was everything I had evisaged; the 'tricorne' hat, the twinkle in the eye, the swift precision of movement. Every remembered intonation was there too, every sharply delivered line, every little gurgle. . . . If, with intense concentration, I could detach myself for a moment from Marie Tempest's personality and performance, I might perhaps see what a tenuous and frivolous little piece *The Marquise* is. I might, if only I could forget her in the last act eating an orange and watching Raoul and Estaban fighting a duel, realize how weak and meretricious the last act is. I might, bereft of her memory, read with disdain the whole play; sneer at its flippancy; laugh at its trivial love scene and shudder at the impertinence of an author who . . . elects to place a brittle modern comedy in an eighteenth-century setting.

Coward, 'Preface' to *Play Parade, Vol. 3*

Semi-Monde

Play: originally entitled *Ritz Bar*.
Written: 1926.
First production: Citizens' Th., Glasgow, 11 Sept. 1977 (dir. and
   des. Philip Prowse; with Citizens' Theatre Company).
Unpublished.

A circular lounge bar of the Ritz Hotel, Paris, is festooned with
balloons and paper streamers. Tall mirrors across the back of the
stage are topped with art deco panels. Beige flower bowls are
brim-full of pink and blue lilacs. A clown in baggy white . . . is
slumped on the floor, while 'Lady Be Good' is played on the
grand piano. A honeymoon couple are squabbling, a group of
fierce ladies, one of them called Inez Zulietta, are in the grip of a
lesbian intrigue, and a Russian who, someone says, has doubtlessly
been eating black bread, is making a nuisance of himself. Semi-
Monde *is written on the scale of* Cavalcade. . . . *The world it*
describes is one of shrieking, bitchy, self-conscious intrigue and
the play is probably the most accurate stage representation of the
twenties milieu Coward inhabited that we have. Two married
couples exchange partners; the band of lesbians are balanced
against the clutch of highly-strung homosexuals; the Russian is
shot dead late in the play by an irate rival called Mike Cavan, and
a sad loner, Cyril Hardacre, wanly pursues one of the married
ladies.

In Philip Prowse's breathtaking production, history is closing in
more rapidly than perhaps Coward knew or intended. A page boy
previously in search of Mrs. Simpson walks through the final
scene calling for 'Madame la Duchesse de Windsor', while Cyril,
now in an RAF uniform confers anxiously with his married lover.
Sirens mingle with Debussy and the hotel vacuum cleaner. The
stage picture is austerely transformed with white streamers and
balloons. The lilacs have been replaced with tiger lilies.

Every now and then there is a moment of vintage Coward.
Jerome Kennedy, an ageing novelist, says good-bye to Tania
Marshall, who is stunningly attired in transparent mauve lace and
fighting back the tears with banal comments about the new hit
revue. And when someone yelps 'Oh God!' as the tension escalates,

he is chided with 'That remark no longer has any dramatic signi-
ficance. One uses it when one can't find a taxi.' The characters
talk about returning to London, being homesick for the South of
France, living for the moment.... The young cast, all thirty of
them, project an *idea* of world-weary insouciance rather than its
embodiment. This is consistent with the company style and
allows for both affection and mockery in the production.

Michael Conveney, *Financial Times*, 12 Sept. 1977

As so often with Coward, it is not so much the people themselves
that grip you as his own equivocal attitude towards them. He was,
by instinct, a puritan dandy with a Martini in one hand and a
moral sampler in the other. And in *Semi-Monde* you can see
clearly that, while he envies the rich their style, he also has the
true lower middle-class boy's belief that a life without work
cannot be pure. Even his attitude to homosexuality is not exactly
encouraging; he seems to suggest it should be practised but not
preached....

Significantly, the one homosexual who earns Coward's
approval is a student-singer who is encouraged to devote himself
to his career. This fits in with Coward's own code of constant
work and sexual discretion.... Mr. Prowse has pushed the later
scenes forward in time so that we get Hitler on the radio, and the
break-up of the glittering tribe. This strikes me as over-literal. The
whole point of Coward in the mid-twenties was that he was
uneasy without being prophetic.

Michael Billington, *The Guardian*, 12 Sept. 1977

The whole action ... took place in the public rooms of the Ritz
Hotel in Paris over a period of three years. It was well-constructed
and, on the whole, well written; its production in London or New
York seemed unlikely as some of the characters, owing to lightly
suggested abnormalities, would certainly be deleted by the
censor; Max Reinhardt, however, was enthusiastic about it, and it
was translated into German by Rudolf Kommer and taken in due
course to Berlin, where for years it escaped production by a
hair's breadth until eventually Vicky Baum wrote *Grand Hotel*,
and *Semi-Monde*, being too closely similar in theme, faded gently
into oblivion.

Coward, *Present Indicative*, p. 277

Home Chat

Play in three acts.
Written: 1927.
First London production: Duke of York's Th., 25 Oct. 1927 (dir.
   Basil Dean; with Madge Titheradge as Janet Ebony and Arthur
   Margetson as Peter Chelsworth).
First New York production: Majestic Th., Brooklyn, 8 Oct. 1934.
Published: London: Secker, 1927; in *Three Plays with a Preface;*
   and in *Play Parade, Vol. 3.*

Janet Ebony is the object of considerable disapproval when she is
wrongly suspected by all of having an affair with Peter Chelsworth
— a suspicion she herself does little to allay. With the truth out
and trust reigning, her husband subsequently refuses to believe
her truthful confession to having an affair with Major Stone.

What is Mr. Coward trying to do in this play? Is this farce or a
comedy or a parody of what are called strong plays? If he is only
up to his fun, and 'codding' the strong, sentimental drama, then
Mr. Basil Dean has not produced the play as satirical farce, nor
does Miss Titheradge act it otherwise than in the spirit of comedy.
Can it be that Mr. Coward did not really know what he was
doing? ... The finest acting was given at the end of the second
act, in a deliciously-written ... scene between Janet and Major
Stone, and in the major part of the third act in which Mr. Coward's
extraordinary facility for inventing audaciously comic situations
was lavishly displayed.

The Observer, 30 Oct. 1927

Home Chat is a light comedy.... The opening performance was
rendered agonizing by one of the more elderly actresses in the
company forgetting her lines continually with the result that the
pauses she made while trying to remember, coupled with the
intentional pauses that Basil Dean had carefully rehearsed,
frequently brought the play to a standstill. There were boos at
the end, and I bounded on to the stage with my usual misguided
valour and had a brisk exchange of unpleasantness with the
gallery. However no good came of it, and the play closed after a
few weeks. I do not think it would have lasted that long had it

not been for the acting of Madge Titheradge.

Coward, 'Preface' to *Play Parade, Vol. 3*

[In response to the question, 'What is your least favourite play?']
I think *Home Chat* is a thin little play. It could have been so
much better. I was awfully cock-a-hoop in those days. I wrote it
without taking enough trouble. When you have a failure, it's
always your fault, nobody else's fault. But actors do a certain
amount of damage.

Coward, interviewed by Edgar Lustgarten,
The Listener, 12 Oct. 1972

This Year of Grace!

Revue.
Written: 1927-28.
First London production: by C.B. Cochran, London Pavilion,
22 Mar. 1928 (book, lyrics, and music by Coward; with
Lance Lister, Douglas Byng, Sonnie Hale, Maisie Gay, and
Jessie Matthews).
First New York production: Selwyn Th., 7 Nov. 1928.
Published: in *Play Parade, Vol. 2;* score by William Chappell,
1928; and selections in *Collected Sketches and Lyrics; The
Noël Coward Song Book;* and *The Lyrics of Noël Coward.*

Such thread of artistic continuity as the mighty assemblage of
varieties has is in the impress of Mr. Noël Coward as composer
and librettist. His music shows an excellent fertility of light ideas.
He turns with equal facility from the sober measure of his 'Mary,
Make Believe' ... to the graceful pizzicato of 'Mad about You',
the highly modish 'blues' rhythm of 'Room with a View' or the
haunting and highly accommodating tune of 'Teach Me to Dance
Like Grandma', which converts itself pleasantly to a waltz. His
book is uneven, but the general level of his humorous verse is
refreshingly high, and in several of his sketches — notably that
which 'pots' four contemporary plays with devastating brevity
and that which tackles a triangle drama in the various manners of
three contemporary playwrights — he scores his points with the
speed and certainty that revue demands. ... There is perhaps
nothing in this revue that quite takes the high aesthetic place of
the Massine choreography of 1926, though such items as the

imaginative 'Lorelei' and the finely set Mexican ballet will be a comparison.

A.S.W., *Manchester Guardian*, 23 Mar. 1928

Quite early in the first half came my series of short one-line parodies on current plays, the final one of the series being announced as 'Any Noël Coward Play'. . . . The scene consisted merely of a row of people, with an author in the centre, bowing, until at a given moment, the leading lady stepped forward, and, with tears in her voice, said 'Ladies and gentleman, this is the happiest moment of my life' [as Frances Doble had done in *Sirocco*], whereupon she burst into sobs and the entire orchestra and any of us in the audience who happened to be in the know, booed and rasperried with the utmost fevour.

The response of the first-nighters to this was interesting. There was first of all dead silence, then a titter of shocked amazement and then a full-bellied roar of laughter.

Coward, *Present Indicative*, p. 332-3

Bitter-Sweet

'An operette.'
Written: 1928-29.
First London production: presented by C.B. Cochran, His
   Majesty's Th., 12 July 1929; trans. Palace Th., 2 Mar. 1931;
   Lyceum Th. 13 Apr. 1931 (dir. Coward; des. Gladys Calthrop
   (London scenes) and Ernst Stern (Vienna scenes); with Peggy
   Wood as the Marchioness of Shayne, George Metaxa as Carl
   Linden, and Ivy St. Helier as Manon La Crevette).
First New York production: Ziegfeld Th., Nov. 1929 (dir.
   Coward; with Evelyn Laye as Lady Shayne).
Film versions: by British and Dominion Films, 1933 (dir. Herbert
   Wilcox; adapt. Wilcox and Monckton Hoffe); and by Metro-
   Goldwyn-Mayer, 1941 (dir. W.S. Van Dyke II; adapt. Lesser
   Samuels).
Published: London: Secker, 1929; London; New York: Samuel
   French, 1923; in *Bitter Sweet and Other Plays*; in *Play Parade,
   Vol. 1;* and in *Plays: Two.*

*Dolly Chamberlain, the well-brought-up English girl of 1929, jilts
her lover to elope with the musician, just as Lady Shayne, who*

found her in his arms, had eloped, fifty-four years ago, from her conventional family, in 1875.

The Sketch, 31 July 1929

A simple little story, but told (after a quiet opening act) with a wealth of light and colour and movement in which scenery, costumes, and music are charmingly blended, the entrancing lilt of Viennese waltzes, grave and gay, ever in the background. . . .

But it was the scene of the Vienna cafe which charmed me most: its plush settees and massed gas globes, its frowsy waiters and bickering band, its company of lively and amorous 'Ladies of the Town', all gave the authentic air of tawdry and slightly disreputable gaiety and high spirits.

And best of all there was Manon, a diminutive *gamine*, clad in shimmering tinsel, and shrieking shrill songs in the *argot* of Montmartre. Miss St Helier's performance is uncannily clever, and her sobs which rent the awed silence at the close of the fatal duet are terribly poignant.

Alan Parsons, *Morning Post,* 18 July 1929

The crash of inarticulate sound at the opening of the acts, the serried ranks of young women and young men who had at intervals to throng the stage, the massed ensembles dragged in as a tribute to tradition and, mistakenly, to the size of His Majesty's Theatre, were all so many concessions to the commonplaceness of popular musical comedy . . . and steps away from the rarer and more delicate form of light opera.

Hubert Griffith, *Evening Standard,* 19 July 1929

Of all the shows I have ever done *Bitter-Sweet* gave me the greatest personal pleasure. My favourite moments were: the finale of the first act when Carl and Sari elope; the café scene when the curtain slowly falls on Carl's death, in a silence broken only by Manon's sobs; the entrance of Madame Sari Linden in her exquisite white dress of the nineties; and, above all, the final moment of the play, when, to the last crashing chords of 'I'll See You Again', Sari, as an old woman, straightens herself with a gesture of indomitable pride and gallantly walks off the stage. . . .

The press notices the next day and on the Sunday following were remarkable for their tone of rather grudging patronage. . . . Some praised the book, but dismissed the music as reminiscent and of no consequence. Some liked the music, but were horrified by the commonplace sentimentality of the book. The lyrics were hardly mentioned, and although the acting and *décor* were favourably received, the general consensus of opinion was that the play would probably run for six weeks or, at the most three months. months.

Coward, *Present Indicative*, p. 353-4

[In reply to the question, which of his plays would he liked best to be remembered?] *Bitter-Sweet*. The reason I say that is because *Bitter-Sweet* combines my talents in almost perfect balance. The dialogue is very good and the music is the best I ever wrote.

Coward, interviewed by Edgar Lustgarten,
The Listener, 12 Oct. 1966

Private Lives

An 'intimate comedy' in three acts.
Written: 1929.
First London production: Phoenix Th., 23 Sept. 1930 (dir. Coward; des. Gladys Calthrop; with Adrianne Allen as Sybil Chase, Coward as Elyot Chase, Laurence Oliver as Victor Prynne, and Gertrude Lawrence as Amanda Prynne).
First New York production: Times Square Th., 27 Jan. 1931.
Revived: Apollo Th., 1 Nov. 1944; Hampsted Th., 24 Apr. 1963, trans. Duke of York's Th., 3 July 1963; Queen's Th., 21 Sept. 1972; Lunt-Fontanne Th., New York, 28 Apr. 1983 (with Richard Burton and Elizabeth Taylor).
Film version: by Metro-Goldwyn-Mayer, 1931 (dir. Sidney Franklin).
Published: London: Heinemann, 1930; London: Samuel French; 1947; in *Play Parade, Vol.1;* and in *Plays: Two*.

On the adjoining balconies of a French hotel are two couples married this morning – Amanda with Victor, Sybil with Elyot. . . . Five years ago Elyot and Amanda were divorced because they loved each other so much that they were forever quarrelling. They meet on the balcony; they discuss two champagne cocktails and the spouses to whom they were this morning linked; they dither, embrace, and flee. That is the first act. . . . In Paris they quarrel, and that is the second act. Next morning Sybil and Victor, having breakfasted, quarrel likewise, and that is the third.

The evening . . . consists in three scenes — a love-scene on the balcony; a bicker and a free fight on a sofa; and another fight . . . among the *débris* of the previous engagement. Marvellously, they are enough. Amanda and Elyot are the fine, flippant flower of Mr. Coward's talent . . . and the dialogue which might seem in print a trickle of inanities becomes in the theatre a perfectly timed and directed interplay of nonsense.

There are moments when even Mr. Coward falters. Before the quarrel reaches its climax the play, because there is nothing else to happen and the author's patter is exhausted, is temporarily converted into a concert party; and again, before breakfast, the patter nearly peters out. But Mr. Coward can pad as no one else can pad; he has made of dramatic upholstery an art.

The Times, 25 Sept. 1930

With Mr. Coward and Miss Gertrude Lawrence to blow the bubbles of caprice and flippancy, the general effect is as light and shiny as can be. . . . Their style is mainly in their clothes; as conversationalists they are mere back-chatterers. . . .

Mr. Coward has the courage of his cunning. He concedes nothing to the old rules of playmaking, of characters, of construction. He trusts to his wits and wins. A little music will help; song for Miss Lawrence and himself. Smashing the furniture is a good old curtain-dropper; so gramophone records are cracked across the pate, and the lamps go down like ninepins. . . . In short, Mr. Coward treats us as children and romps through a charade, knowing also that romping is a fine art and needs to be done 'just so'. . . . Nothing would persuade me to read it in cool and solitary silence.

Ivor Brown, *The Observer*, 29 Sept. 1930

It was an interesting play to play, naturally more interesting for Gertie and me than it was for Larry and Adrianne. We had the parts, or rather, the part, as Elyot and Amanda are practically synonymous. The play's fabric was light and required light handling. Gertie was brilliant. Everything she had been in my mind when I originally conceived the idea in Tokio came to life on the stage: the witty, quicksilver delivery of lines; the romantic quality, tender and alluring; the swift, brittle rages, even the white Molyneux dress.

Coward, Present Indicative, p. 395

It is a reasonably well-constructed duologue for two experienced performers, with a couple of extra puppets thrown in to assist the plot and to provide contrast. There is a well-written love scene in Act I, and a certain amount of sound sex psychology underlying the quarrel scenes in Act II.

As a complete play, it leaves a lot to be desired, principally owing to my dastardly and conscienceless behaviour towards Sybil and Victor, the secondary characters ... but, at any rate, from the point of view of technical acting, it is very interesting indeed.

To begin with, there is no further plot and no further action after Act I, with the exception of the rough-and-tumble fight at the curtain of Act II. Before this, there is exactly forty minutes of dialogue between the leading protagonists, Amanda and Elyot, which naturally demands from them the maximum resource and comedy experience, as every night, according to the degree of responsiveness from the audience, the attack and tempo of the performance must inevitably vary. . . .

Coward, 'Introduction' to Play Parade, Vol. 1

I find that about *Private Lives* I wrote fourteen years ago: 'Whether the people in this play are vile or virtuous is not the touchstone here; they have a butterfly melancholy, and the only question is whether the playwright has given that melancholy its butterfly texture'. Which only shows what nonsense one is capable of. I saw this play a month or two ago performed in a wooden hut somewhere in Sussex to an audience not, one thinks, appreciative of butterflies. The piece had been broadened a little and what texture there was left was that of a flea-bitten hunter's hide. And it brought the roof down, and everybody voted it to be tremendous fun, and during the row on the sofa, the audience stamped and whistled, and shouted, 'Go to it, Elyot!', 'Slosh 'im, Amanda!' I find that in 1930 I talked of this play's 'world-weary banter'. I ought to have had my brains taken out and buttered and given to a dog.

James Agate, Sunday Times, 5 Nov. 1944

In this production . . . Amanda − bright, blithe Amanda − is a middle-aged Kewpie doll with a fishmonger's temper. And Elyot − dapper, quick Elyot − could just as easily be the mortician in *Winesburg, Ohio*. To see Taylor flop down impetuously on a divan, the pants of her pink lounging outfit riding up her calves, is not an edifying sight. To see him hoist himself back up is even less so. Watching Burton hunch-shouldered and stiff as if with arthritis, hobble jauntily across the stage is, quite frankly, painful.

Even worse is what they do to Coward's quicksilver repartee. Burton speaks it for the most part as if it were not quite worthy of him. The words appear to be sullying his mouth and the effortless superiority of Elyot registers in his performance as sour disdain. Taylor, on the contrary, pounces on her punchlines like a beggar on a purse, screws up her face shamelessly, and distends her vowels so that simple adjectives like 'delightful' and 'ugly' sound like howls of pain. Between them, there is no rapport, no unspoken subtext, no glimmer of ambivalent emotion. What you see is what you get.

David Richards, *Washington Post*, 22 Aug. 1974

It's a nice play, *Private Lives*, I'm very fond of it. Of course, the thing about the play which went unobserved at the time is that it is the lightest of light comedies, based on a serious situation which is two people who love each other too much. I wouldn't say it's a tragedy, but there's a sadness below it. . . . I hit Laurence Olivier on the head to make him play Victor, because it isn't really a very good part; but I wanted not to have him cast as an ordinary . . . stuffed-shirt. I said, 'I must have somebody who's physically very attractive, otherwise Amanda would never have married him'.

Coward, interviewed by Michael MacOwen in *Great Acting, The Listener*, 7 Apr. 1966

Some Other Private Lives

Playlet in one act: parody of *Private Lives*.
Written: 1930.
First performed: London Hippodrome, 8 Dec. 1930 (dir. Coward; with Coward, Adrianne Allen, Laurence Oliver, and Gertrude Lawrence in parodies of their *Private Lives* roles).
Revived: by the Noël Coward Co., 1 Sept. 1932, Festival Theatre, Malvern (as afterpiece to *Private Lives*).

Published: in *Collected Sketches and Lyrics* (for two characters only).

Fred and Floss conduct a working-class version of the love-hate relationship between Elyot and Amanda, ending up fighting on the floor of their shabby sitting-room.

Post-Mortem

Play in eight scenes.
Written: 1930.
First professional production: BBC2 TV, 17 Sept. 1968, in 'The Jazz Age' drama series (dir. John MacKenzie).
Published: London: Heinemann, 1931; in *Play Parade, Vol. 1;* and in *Plays: Two.*

It is evident from the text that, though cast in dramatic form, the play has not been calculated in terms of the practical theatre: in particular, there is a scene of confrontation between young selves and mature selves thirteen years later which would be almost impossible to stage. . . . Television should be the ideal medium for the play, which is really written almost as a television play before its time. Television can, or should be able to, manage admirably the transitions between the trenches in 1917, where the hero is dying, and London in 1930, to which he is flashed forward for a bitterly ironic view of the brave new world he has been killed to defend. Unfortunately it was hard to tell in this production whether the play would have worked or not. The 'Jazz Age' series is confined to a fifty-minute slot, which means that most stage plays, and this in particular, have to be cut by at least half in order to fit in. The result here was a breathless jumble, suggesting an arbitrary collection of isolated highlights from a play, rather than the play itself. . . . Even so, moments of power came over, particularly in the hero's meetings with his mother and his fiancee, now long married to someone else.

John Russell Taylor, *Plays and Players,* Nov. 1968

I wrote an angry little vilification of war called *Post-Mortem;* my mind was strongly affected by *Journey's End,* and I had read several current war novels one after the other. I wrote *Post-Mortem* with the utmost sincerity; this, I think, must be fairly obvious to anyone who reads it. In fact I tore my emotions to shreds over it. The result was similar to my performance as Stanhope: [in *Journey's End*, Victoria Theatre, Singapore, 1930, for three guest performances. See *Present Indicative* p. 385-6] confused, under-rehearsed and hysterical. Unlike my performance as Stanhope, however, it had some very fine moments. There is, I believe, some of the best writing I have ever done in it, also some of the worst.

Coward, *Present Indicative*, p. 390-1

[See also 'Preface' to *Play Parade, Vol. 1*; *The Life of Noël Coward* p. 156; and *Diaries,* 12 Feb. 1956.]

Cavalcade

Play in three parts of 22 scenes.
Written: 1930-31.
First London production: Theatre Royal, Drury Lane, 13 Oct. 1931 (dir. Coward; des. Gladys Calthrop; with Mary Clare as Jane Marryot, Edward sinclair as Robert Marryot, Fred Groves as Alfred Bridges, and Una O'Connor as Ellen Bridges).
Revived: Redgrave Theatre, Farnham, Apr. 1981.
First film version: by Fox Film Co., 1932 (dir. Frank Lloyd; adapt. Reginald Berkeley).
Published: in serial form in *Daily Mail,* 10-23 Dec. 1931; London: Heinemann, 1932; selections in *The Noël Coward Song Book* and *The Lyrics of Noël Coward;* in *Play Parade Vol. 1;* and in *Plays: Three.*

Mr. Noël Coward ... has looked at the present century chiefly through the eyes of a woman. She greets the new year with champagne. ... Her husband goes off to South Africa, but she can scarcely bring herself to believe in the reality of war. The tune of 'Dolly Gray' that the band is playing on the quayside seems to confirm her doubts, it is so human and jolly. And on Mafeking night she has a box at the theatre. ... Her husband returns, and the whole family watches the end of the long Victorian day as the Queen's funeral passes through London. After that we march with this woman into the deepening shadows. Her son and his wife are making love on the deck of a liner; a sudden searchlight plays on the liner's name. It is the Titanic. Petticoat Lane . . . serves only to show how war may turn a good butler into a drunken husband. And then the war, with shadowy men marching and singing, and music-hall beauties, more and more hysterical as the years pass, scream their erotic recruiting songs. Armistice brings to the central figure of this nightmare the telegram which tells her that her only son has been killed, but she joins the crowds in Trafalgar-square, and – half-despairingly, half-defiantly – flourishes a rattle. The world grows gay and heartless again, but . . . it is a fierce gaiety, a cruel carelessness. We leave the woman lifting her glass against a background of crisis and confusion to the hope that England may regain her dignity and greatness.

The Times, 14 Oct. 1931

Chelsea and Bloomsbury, foregathering in the foyer, made no secret of the fact that this production had not their approval. Stage-pictures, they said, did not make a play; there was no wit, and such stirring of the emotions as they detected was obviously vulgar. . . . [But] Mr. Coward's job was to bethink himself of Drury Lane Theatre . . . which holds 2600 people, nine times a week, for fifty-two weeks. . . . Mr. Coward had the happy idea of presenting as drama to the eye the principal events of the last thirty years. But since Drury Lane stage does not revolve, he was compelled, while the big scenes were being set, to have little front scenes of narrative value. . . . The scenes which aroused the greatest excitement . . . are Mafeking Night at the theatre, Petticoat Lane, the front at Brighton with the band playing *The Gondoliers*, and the crowd startled by what must surely be Blériot's monoplane, a picture of Waterloo Station during the tragic years, and last, Armistice Night in Trafalgar Square.

James Agate, *Sunday Times*, 13 Oct. 1931

It is not just spectacle for eye-dazzling sake. There is always a point of view. . . . As a special stroke of swift, dramatic economy consider the rendering of 1914-1918. Behind is a mounting procession of soldiers, patient, reiterant, plodding eternally in a fog of war; in front the comediennes sing their patriotic songs, at first jauntily . . . and then, with the passing years and growing strain, they sing wearily, and a pale, self-flogging fever of animation. . . .

Mr. Coward mixes sympolism with realism. . . . But of all the multitudinous impressions there remain . . . a small voice here (the children asking about Queen Victoria, and eyeing the cake), or perhaps a single drunken scream, like that of the unseen woman, a laughing Hyaena on the night of 4 August 1914, or again one of those dim figures in the murk of Victoria Station four years of anguish later. . . . . The waltz comingles with the dirge and the double shuffle of the minstrel boys with the tramp of those who to the wars have gone. . . .

Ivor Brown, *The Observer,* 13 Oct. 1931

We planned the production so that there should be never more than thirty seconds' wait between any of its twenty-three scenes. The stage was divided into six hydraulic lifts. These had to be timed to sink and rise on light cues from the prompt corner; at the same moment, other light cues would cause the hanging parts of the scenery to be whisked up into the flies and simultaneously replaced. We installed a row of automatic lights along the front of the second balcony. These had five changes of colour and could be regulated by electricians from the stage. The foot-lights were reconstructed so that they could silently disappear altogether for the big scenes, and rise into place again for the small interiors when needed.

Coward, *Present Indicative,* p. 402-3

Everybody seemed to be more concerned with *Cavalcade* as a patriotic appeal than as a play. This attitude I realized had been enhanced by my first-night speech — 'A pretty exciting thing to be English' — quite true, quite sincere; I felt it strongly, but I rather wished I hadn't said it, hadn't popped it on top of *Cavalcade* like a paper cap. I hadn't written the play on a dashing patriotic appeal at all. There was certainly a love of England in it, but primarily it was the story of thirty years in the life of a family.

Coward, *Present Indicative,* p. 412

By brilliant use of an open stage, and an even more brilliant deal with Equity whereby only a dozen of the cast have to be professionals (the rest all drawn from local amateur groups). Farnham has achieved the impossible. . . . For the first time in the theatregoing life of anyone much under 60, we get the change to look at the most ambitious stage concept put together by a

British playwright this century.... In reversing the last two scenes, so that we end not with the cynical 'Twentieth Century Blues' but with the jingoistic toast 'To England' and a mass singing of 'Land of Hope and Glory', [the director] has perhaps left us with a false impression of *Cavalcade* as a work of mindless partiotism instead of as a rather more complex hymn of love and hate to Britain.

Sheridan Morley, *International Herald Tribune*, 23 Apr. 1981

Words and Music

Revue.
Written: 1932.
First London production: by C.B. Cochran, Adelphi Th., 16 Sept. 1932 (book, lyrics, and music by Coward; dir. Coward; des. Gladys Calthrop; with Ivy St. Helier and Joyce Barvour).
First New York production: as *Set to Music* (revised and re-written 1938), Music Box Th., 18 Jan. 1939 (with Beatrice Lillie, Richard Haydn, and Moya Nugent).
Published: London: Chappell, 1932 (vocal score); in *Play Parade, Vol. 2;* and selections in *The Lyrics of Noël Coward* and *The Noël Coward Song Book.*

Mr. Coward has, above all else, the gift of satire, and this revue, being primarily satirical, is his best work in the musical kind. There have been occasions in the past when his satire has degenerated into a thin, repellant sourness — a condition to be observed even now in 'Something to Do with Spring' which is the evening's unique failure. But in this revue his satirical pieces have nearly always the active fierceness which is the distinction between genuine satire and empty sneering and they have too, though divided in subject, the unity of a single purpose. 'Mad About the Boy', a study of feminine enslavement to a film star, has even pity to enforce its thrust; a burlesque of spectacular play-production which ... bitterly applies the method of *Casanova* to the subject of *Journey's End*, has a just and slashing cruelty; and 'Midnight Matinèe', though it has a seemingly gentler touch, exhibits without much reserve and with a splendidly inventive humour the weary, muddled, dismal exhibitionism of a group that must for ever be aping Lady Godiva or Nell Gwynne or Salome in the sacred cause of their own boredom. Lady Godiva shambles across the stage in a rush of absurd modesty; Nell spills her apples and

Salome dances among them. [But] ... Mr. Coward, when he forsakes satire and writes as other men do for revues, writes only a little better than they, and such brief essays in sentimentality as 'Let's Say Good-Bye' are not comfortable, though even they have generally a sting that saves them from dullness.

The Times, 17 Sept. 1932

Design for Living

Comedy in three acts.

Written: 1932.

First London production: Haymarket Th., 25 Jan. 1939; trans. Savoy Th., 13 June 1939 (dir. Harold French; des. Roger K. Furse; with Diana Wynyard as Gilda, Anton Walbrook as Otto, and Rex Harrison as Leo).

First New York production: Ethel Barrymore Th., 24 Jan. 1933 (dir. Coward; des. Gladys Calthrop; with Lynn Fontanne as Gilda, Alfred Lunt as Otto, and Coward as Leo).

Revived: Phoenix Th., 21 Nov. 1973 (dir. Michael Blakemore; with Vanessa Redgrave, Jeremy Brett, and John Stride); Globe Th., 4 Aug. 1983 (dir. Alan Strachan; with Maria Aitken, Ian Ogilvy, and Gary Bond).

Film version: by Paramount, 1933 (dir. Ernst Lubitsch; adapt. Ben Hecht).

Published: New York: Doubleday, 1933; London: Heinemann, 1933; in *Six Plays;* in *Play Parade, Vol. 1;* and in *Plays: Three.*

What [Mr. Coward] really enjoys is the bizarre nonsense of his three characters. One is a playwright. One is an artist. The third is a woman who is also an artist. Otto and Leo, who are close friends of very long standing, both love her very much, and she loves them. To save herself from the complications of this singular situation, she escapes from both and marries a sober art merchant who takes her to New York. But after a voyage round the world on a freighter, the two wild oats turn up ... at her penthouse apartment. Their impudent gaiety disarms her. After a stormy session with her husband, who knows the code of a gentleman, she returns to the exuberant disorder of her kind.

Unfortunately for the uses of artificial comedy, establishing this triangular situation involves considerable sobriety. All through the first act, Mr. Coward writes as earnestly as a psychologist. Through a long stretch of the third act he surrenders entirely to the patter of ordinary folk and, incidentally, to ordinary actors who can make little of the wrangling impertinence of their lines. When *Design for Living* sounds serious, you wish impatiently that Mr. Coward would cut the cackle and come to the main business, which is his brand of satire and comedy. He touches that off with remarkable dexterity: Otto and Leo striding pompously around Gilda's penthouse in the last act. The fluff of wordly success and the vaudeville of telephone conversations suit Mr. Coward's skimming pen exactly. When he is in an impish mood, which is most of the time, he is enormously funny.

Brooks Atkinson, *New York Times*, 25 Jan. 1933

The story leaves one with an uncomfortable feeling that it starts too late and ends too soon. . . . In the first two acts we see Otto and Leo almost exclusively in a state of jealous antagonism, so that when, in the third act, these two old lovers break in on Gilda's respectable marriage with amiable impudence which wins her heart by reviving dear old times, what Mr. Coward is doing is to revive old times with which the audience has had no previous acquaintance. So far as we are concerned Otto and Leo have suddenly become new characters. We should have seen them behaving after this fashion in happy circumstances earlier in the evening, which is what I mean when I say that the comedy starts too late.

And it ends too soon too because when Gilda . . . brings down the curtain by going off to live with both Otto and Leo in a *ménage à trois*, we feel that we have reached the really interesting part of the story.

Herbert Farjeon, *The Bystander*, 8 Feb. 1939

Sexual manners may have caught up with the play in the 1960s, but its popularity now may have more to do with a new generation clutching for the style of the 1930s. . . . For its move from the Greenwich Theatre to the Globe, Alan Strachan has made very few changes in his production, but none the less the centre has shifted. Maria Aitken portrays Gilda in much the same languorous style as before, flashing quick jokes and rueful comments. . . . Now, however, every consideration of her actions is visible in her face and voice. . . . It becomes a play about liberations in matters other than sexual.

The surprisingly fine partnership of Gary Bond and Ian Ogilvy ... is still strong, but the hilarity of their drunk scene and their appearance as twins when they arrive in the third act to reclaim her from her new husband now has additional solidity. It has been provided for them by Miss Aitken's assumption of power. Because they, too, have to change to accept that the three of them share an unusual bond of love, the sense of liberation is infectious.

Ned Chaillet, *The Times*, 5 Aug. 1983

Design for Living as a project rather than a play sat patiently at the back of my mind for eleven years. It had to wait until Lynn Fontanne, Alfred Lunt, and I had arrived, by different roads, at the exact moment in our careers when we felt that we could all three play together with a more or less equal degree of success. ... I never intended for a moment that the design for living suggested in the play should apply to anyone outside its three principal characters. ... These glib, over-articulate, and amoral creatures force their lives into fantastic shapes and problems because they cannot help themselves. Impelled chiefly by the impact of their personalities each upon the other, they are like moths in a pool of light, unable to tolerate the lonely outer darkness, and equally unable to share the light without colliding constantly and bruising one another's wings.

The end of the play is equivocal. The three of them, after various partings and reunions and partings again, after torturing and loving and hating one another, are left together as the curtain falls, laughing. Different minds found different meanings in this laughter. Some considered it to be directed against Ernest, Gilda's husband and the time-honoured friend of all three. If so, it was certainly cruel, and in the worst possible taste. Some saw it as a lascivious anticipation of a sort of triangular carnal frolic. Others, with less ribald imaginations, regarded it as a meaningless and slightly inept excuse to bring the curtain down. I as the author, however, prefer to think that Gilda and Otto and Leo were laughing at themselves.

Coward, 'Introduction' to *Play Parade, Vol. 1*

Conversation Piece

A 'romantic comedy with music' in three acts.
Written: 1933.

First London production: His majesty's Th., 16 Feb. 1934 (dir. Coward; des. Gladys Calthrop; with Yvonne Printemps as Melanie and Coward as Paul).

First New York production: 44th Street Th., 23 Oct. 1934.

Published London: Heinemann, 1934; London: Chappell, 1934 (vocal score); in *Play Parade, Vol. 2;* and in *Plays: Three.*

Mr. Coward plays a French duke, exiled during the revolution and now turned adventurer. Mlle. Printemps is his ward, a young singer whom he has picked out of the Paris gutter and is now trying to foist on a sceptical Brighton as his aristocratic ward, so that she shall make a rich marriage and he pouch the proceeds. Of course, the Duke and the singer fall in love and end in one another's arms. Equally, of course, this is the oldest and most sentimental story in the world. But, told with such grace, here is room for it to be told again. . . .

W.A. Darlington, *Daily Telegraph*, 17 Feb. 1934

A confused affair about a couple of French adventurers whose twists and turns were too much for me. The curtain dropped on the second act with the female adventurer declaring her passionate love for her partner in the presence of everybody in the cast, and rose on the third act with the young woman's lips glued to those of an English marquis. Which caused the adventurer to say: 'A trifle vulgar after the scene you made last night!' It was more than vulgar; it was not to be understood. . . . The piece, as was to be expected in a play that obviously started in band-box vein, is full of tiny strokes of admirable craftmanship. Things like the first scene, in which no word is spoken and the intensive silence keys up the audience to a giddy expectation. Things like the party scene, which is conceived in the form of a dance. Here, whenever anyone speaks the dancers suspend animation like the figures on a clock that has done striking. . . . The wit, when we are allowed any, is . . . at once unexpected, mordant, and bitter-sweet. . . . . .

James Agate, *Sunday Times,* 19 Feb. 1934

Mr. Coward has been more concerned to provide a medium for Mlle. Printemps than to prepare a balanced play. . . . With her little shrugs and nods and the action of a shoulder-blade which can point to silence a sentence with magical effect, [she] carries the play along as a solo performance, whenever there is need. The play does need some carrying, for it strolls . . . from ducal lodging to the lawns or the reception-room and back again without offering much opportunity for concerted acting.

Ivor Brown, *The Observer*, 19 Feb. 1934

Point Valaine

Play in three acts.
Written: 1934.
First London production: Embassy Th., Swiss Cottage, 3 Sept. 1947 (dir. Peter Glenville; des. Tanya Moiseiwitsch; with Mary Ellis as Linda Valaine, Ben-Astar as Stefan, Anthony Ireland as Mortimer Quinn, and Allan Cuthbertson as Martin Welford).
First New York production: Ethel Barrymore Th., 16 Jan. 1935 (dir. Coward; des. Gladys Calthrop; with Lynn Fontanne as Linda, Alfred Lunt as Stefan, Osgood Perkins as Quinn, and Louis Hayward as Welford).
Published: New York: Doubleday, 1935; London: Heinemann, 1935; in *Six Plays of Today* (London: Heinemann, 1939); in *Curtain Calls;* and in *Play Parade, Vol. 6.*

A wholly unsmiling picture of lust and rough manners in a tropical setting. . . . The simple story has the ring of truth, and its central character is portrayed full length, full depth. She is a middle-aged hotel keeper on an isolated island who permits herself a sordid passion in which a shambling animalistic head waiter is her companion. A wholesome and idealistic English aviator arrives on the scene. He and the woman fall romantically in love with each other, and their idyll is brutally shattered when the waiter returns unexpectedly from a trip to the mainland. The intruder man-handles his former mistress and throws himself to the sharks. . . .

For all its rather calculated violence the scene holds, and should communicate the pathos of a woman who is time's fool. If in this performance the pathos is suggested rather than communicated the fault would not seem to be in the writing. Some passages, no doubt, are emotionally overwrought, but their weakness is unduly stressed by the sluggish pace of the acting. Miss Mary Ellis, as the hotel keeper, scarcely conveys the state of high tension at which the woman is living when she is induced to yield herself to a romantic love which she knows has come too late, and the scene of her surrender, though every line reveals a new aspect of her problem, lacking the necessary tension, seems long and laboured.

The Times, 4 Sept. 1947

Once the decorations, racial and climatic, have been stripped, we are left with a harsh melodrama of one woman, two men. . . . There could be pathos in the figure of a fading woman in her St Martin's summer; in the tragedy of a late-flowering love. But Coward . . . has fumbled his words: those that he finds baffle even the art of Mary Ellis, who does what tact and technique can achieve for a part scrawled in grease-paint. Happily, there are gleams of the other, wittier Coward — expressed in the irony of the peripatetic novelist who is for a moment a guest at the hotel, peeping and botanizing with a grim pleasure that has begun to fray into boredom.

The Observer, 7 Sept. 1947

To-Night at 8.30

Ten one-act plays, forming three programmes of three in varying combinations. *We Were Dancing, The Astonished Heart, Red Peppers, Hands Across The Sea, Fumed Oak, Shadow Play, Family Album, Star Chamber, Ways and Means, Still Life.*
Written: 1935-36.
First London production: Phoenix Th., Jan. 1936. First programme, 9 Jan., with *Family Album, The Astonished Heart,* and *Red Peppers;* second programme, 13 Jan., with *Hands Across the Sea, Fumed Oak,* and *Shadow Play;* the other plays being introduced into repertoire to give three groups of there plays, with the exception of *Star Chamber*, which played on 21 March only (dir. Coward; des. Glayds Calthrop; with Coward, Gertrude Lawrence, Alan Webb, and Alison Leggat).
First American production: National Th., New York, 24 Nov. 1936, in three programmes (dir. Coward; des. Gladys Calthrop; with Coward and Gertrude Lawrence).
Revived: Fortune Th., 20 Jan. 1971 (dir. Gillian Lynne; with Millicent Martin, Alan MacNaughtan, Gary Bond, and Joyce Grant).
Film versions: as *Meet Me To-Night, (Red Peppers, Fumed Oak,*

and *Ways and Means),* by Anthony Havelock Allen Productions, 1952 (dir. Anthony Pelissier; *We Were Dancing,* by MGM, 1942 (dir. Robert Z. Leonard; adapt. West, Rameau, and Froeschel); *Still Life,* as *Brief Encounter,* by Cineguild, 1945 (dir. David Lean; adapt. and prod. Coward); *The Astonished Heart,* by Gainsborough Pictures, 1950 (dir. Terence Fisher and Anthony Darnborough; adapt. Coward).

Published: London; Heinemann, 1936, in three volumes; in *Curtain Calls;* London; New York: Samuel French, 1938; *Brief Encounter* in *Three British Screenplays,* ed. Roger Manvell (London: Methuen, 1950); selections in *The Lyrics of Noël Coward;* in *Play Parade, Vol. 4;* and in *Plays: Three (Hands Across the Sea, Still Life,* and *Fumed Oak)* and *Plays: Four (Ways and Means, The Astonished Heart,* and *Red Peppers).*

Family Album is a funereal jollity with music. The scene, dated 1860, and charmingly decorated by Mrs. Calthrop, is a background to a family of that period, weeping over their dead father and swerving, in Mr. Coward's most uncomfortable manner, from sadness to fooling, from fooling to sentimentality, and from sentimentality to high-jinks with the butler. To be on the safe side, the tears are sugared and the sentiments acidulated, but when, at length, all is said and done, the apologies to *Bitter-Sweet* are found to be insufficient.

The *Astonished Heart* is at any rate a serious attempt to write a serious play. . . . Mr. Coward's purpose is to exhibit the tyranny of the body over the mind and the humiliation of a spirit tormented and confused. He himself is the husband; Miss Leggatt, with feeling and distinction, is the wife; Miss Gertrude Lawrence is the woman whose subject he becomes. The writing and performance are successful up to a point; they create a genuine nervous tension that is clearly related to the tension of tragedy; but tragedy, though strained for, does not come. Mr. Coward's people of the theatre can quarrel brilliantly, can play upon each other's nerves, and communicate their jangled distress, but they do not suffer. . . . They are too active, too glib, too adroit, too easily poised, but, above all, too conscious of their audience. Miss Lawrence lying on her face on the floor and Mr. Coward leaping from the balcony have not the dignity of tragic climax. But the thing is courageous and not frivolous, not written to be popular. At one moment, when Mr. Coward carefully looks at his face in the mirror going to his death, it has a genuinely imaginative pang.

But the theatrical success of the evening belongs without

question to the *Red Peppers*, a music-hall pair, in their dressing-room and on the stage. Here, with quarrels and back-chat, Mr. Coward the dramatist is comfortably within his range, and Mr. Coward, the actor and, above all, the dancer, knows how, with Miss Lawrence, to make the most of his own swift nonsense. It was a robust end to an otherwise slim or perilous entertainment.

The Times, 10 Jan. 1936

As a second-rate entertainment, *To-Night at Eight-Thirty* proved to have its points.... Out of three short plays by Mr. Noël Coward included under this title, the most popular was *Red Peppers*, in which he wore a sailor suit and a red nose.

Naturally, in the same way as Mr. Shaw would be a success if he cared to appear on the halls as a tramp-cyclist, this brought the evening to a happy conclusion.

Daily Mail, 10 Jan. 1930

[*Shadow Play*] is a fantasy to which it is difficult to attune the mind after the comedies which precede it, and perhaps its proper place is the first in the programme instead of last.... Victoria Gayforth takes an overdose of her sleeping draught, and we have presented to us in a series of scenes, the confused pictures and memories that flit through her distraught mind.... Unfortunately, they come across the footlights still considerably confused, and there are scraps of dialogue which should be passionate and intense, but these lack conviction, principally owing to their scrappiness, which is not a very happy medium for the expression of sincere feeling.

The Bystander, 5 Feb. 1936

[*Ways and Means* is] an airy trifle about an attractive young couple who are living a gay life entirely beyond their means, and employing ways which are not beyond reproach to replenish their funds.... Noël Coward and Gertrude Lawrence as the Cartwrights indulge in a great deal of bright chat with an occasional spot of rough and tumble. It all amounts to very little, but in spite of that it is amusing and was received by the audience with much hilarity.

In ... *Still Life*, the author is not altogether successful. He writes this time about an ordinary couple ... but he paints them in unnecessarily dull colours. ... These meet by chance in the restaurant room of a railway station, and we see them meeting there at intervals during the year that their romance lasts. Actually, it is rather a sordid little affair and not so pathetically tragic as Noël Coward, with his persuasive dialogue, tries to make us believe. The proceedings are much enlivened by the doing of the station staff, particularly the 'refeened' barmaid excellently played by Joyce Carey.

The Bystander, 10 June 1936

Of the Three, *We Were Dancing* still looks emphatically the best. Dismissed by Coward as little more than a curtain-raiser, it actually provides a marvellously compact illustration of the way the English public school spirit prevails even in moments of strenuous passion. On a verandah somewhere East of Suez an eloping couple are confronted by the girl's immaculately polite husband; but the irony is that the bond between her husband and the lover proves to be the strongest link in the emotional chain, and that supposedly uncontrollable urges are described in language full of precise, decorous understatement. . . .

Red Peppers, Coward's hymn to the tatty world of twice-nightly variety, also works simply because the action is carefully rooted in a vanished theatrical past: a world in which legit actors rubbed shoulders with stand-up comics, top liners fell down drunk at the Empire, Hartlepool, and Garbo was only dismissed because she'd never be able to hold a Saturday-night audience at Davenport.

Only *Family Album*, blending mild satire on Victorian hypocrisy with candid exploitation of the period's sentimentality now looks as if it's being kept alive by the cast's and the director's artificial respiration.

Michael Billington, *The Times*, 21 Jan. 1971

Operette

Musical comedy in two acts.
Written: 1937.
First London production: His Majesty's Th., 16 Mar. 1938 (dir. Coward; des. Gladys Calthrop; with Peggy Wood as Rozanne Gray, Griffith Jones as Nigel Vaynham Fritzi Massary as Liesl Haren, and Irene Vanbrugh as the Countess of Messiter).
Published: London: Heinemann, 1938; London: Chappell, 1938 (score); selections in *The Noël Coward Song Book* and *The*

Lyrics of Noël Coward; and in *Play Parade, Vol. 2.*

The story . . . is all about a musical comedy actress who refused to marry the heir to a peerage because he would have to resign his commission.

This is trite. . . . The *milieu* is the lighter stage of 1906, and Mr. Coward should know without my telling him that the musical comedies of that period were nothing like so dull as *The Model Maid* pretends to be. He should know this if only because he wrote the 'Mirabelle' scene in *Cavalcade.* Does Mr. Coward really think that this present backstage quarrelling is a patch on the same thing in *Red Peppers?* . . . I doubt even whether Mr. Coward's tunes are as good as they used to be. . . .

James Agate, Sunday Times, 16 Mar. 1938

Mr. Coward, a lover of the theatre for its own sake, has been fascinated by the idea and the scenic opportunity of enclosing a play within a play — a musical comedy of 1906, the rigidity of which he can burlesque, within a backstage story of the same date. . . . The trouble is that the enclosed burlesque is conspicuously less gay than the entertainment it guys, for the Edwardian musical comedy stage knew its business: and that the external story of the nobleman and the chorus-girl, with its customary deeds of self-sacrifice, is in itself so commonplace that all the scene-shifters and dressmakers in the world cannot make it suffice for three hours.

The Times, 17 Mar. 1938

Operette from my point of view is the least successful musical play I have ever done. The reason for this is that it is over-written and under-composed. The story . . . while not fiercely original, is an agreeable enough background for gay music and lyrics and beguiling 'period' costumes. Unfortunately however the plot which should have been the background became the foreground, and the music, which should have dominated the action, established the atmosphere and whirled the play into a lilting success, was meagre and, only at moments, adequate. . . . The only real lyric success of the entertainment was 'The Stately

Homes of England' which had very little connection with the story. . . .

Another aspect of *Operette* was the triumphant confusion it established in the minds of the audience. This was cunningly achieved by the switching of the action back and forth between the stage play and the real play. I remember peering from by box . . . and watching bewildered playgoers rustling their programmes and furtively striking matches in a frantic effort to discover where they were and what was going on . . . .

Coward, 'Introduction' to *Play Parade, Vol. 2*

Present Laughter

Light comedy in three acts.

Written: 1939.

First London production: alternately with *This Happy Breed*, Haymarket Th., 29 Apr. 1943 (dir. Coward; des. Gladys Calthrop; with Coward as Garry Essendine, Joyce Carey as Liz Essendine; Jennifer Gray as Daphne Stillington, Judy Campbell as Joanna Lyppiatt, Beryl Measor as Monica Reed).

First American production: Plymouth Th., 29 Oct. 1946.

Revived: Haymarket Th., 16 Apr. 1947 (dir. Coward); as *Joyeux Chagrins*, Th. Edouard VII, Paris 17 Nov. 1948 (dir. Coward); Queen's Th., Apr. 1965 (with Nigel Patrick); Royal Exchange Th., Manchester, 31 Mar. 1977 (dir. James Maxwell; with Albert Finney); Vaudeville Th., 17 Mar. 1981 (dir. Alan Strachan; with Donald Sinden*)*.

Published: London: Heinemann, 1943; London and New York: Samuel French, 1949; in *Play Parade, Vol. 4;* and in *Plays: Four.*

The principal characters are a middle-aged actor, his amiably separated wife, and the peculiar people who feed his vanity. The time is the giddy nineteen-twenties. The framework is a series of highly unconventional situations; the material is the self-centered affections and affectations of so many peacocks. . . .

Daily Mail, 30 Apr. 1943

To be a talented actor of immense popularity, to have in private life a charm which one cannot help using a little unscrupulously, always to be watching oneself go by — that is the plight of

Garry Essendine, and Mr. Coward plays the character as a man who is aware of his own temperamental sentimentality and masks it whenever possible with a defensive frivolity.... In the first movement of the comedy Mr. Coward sketches Essendine to the life, but even while this brilliant sketch of the artist whose art has ludicrously overwhelmed his life is growing the mock farce is making an amusing beginning. But undoubtedly the best moment is when the practical man of today's theatre rages at the futility of a half-baked highbrowism superbly represented by Mr. James Donald, whose uncouth young man is slightly mad and devastatingly in earnest. The second act sees the wittily impudent and extemely well-invented French farce in full swing, and Mr. Coward and a most amenable Miss Judy Campbell together bring it to a brilliant climax with a mocking variation on the conventional seduction scene. The last act − less good than the others, but not injuriously so − is largely dismissive and Essendine's defence of the frivolous attitude to sex is an inconsistency to those who had felt in the early part of the play that there was some moral integrity of which the actor was cheating the man.

The Times, 30 Apr. 1943

Present Laughter is a very light comedy and was written with the sensible object of providing me with a bravura part. It was an enormous success. I received excellent notices and, to my bewilderment and considerable dismay, the play also was reasonably acclaimed. This so unnerved me that I can say no more.

Coward, 'Introduction' to *Play Parade, Vol. 4*

Aside from the stark contrast between the romantic comedian of Coward's self portrait and this heavily butch reincarnation, the point about Garry is that he is a wholetime actor, on and off stage, invariably taken in by his own performance. As Finney plays him, it is as though Lucky Jim had wound up in Number One dressing room, retaining all his old defensive armoury of funny faces and joke voices, warding off ghastly people with strenuous role-playing, and invariably keeping a sharp eye on the effect he is making no matter how far he goes over the top....

On its last West End showing Nigel Patrick settled for the briskly debonair approach. In Mr. Maxwell's version this changes to a rhythm of relaxation and frenzy. At every ring of the door-bell Rosalind Knight's hump-backed Miss Erikson comes sprinting over the acres of the Exchange floor; and if the visitor happens to be Michael Feast's Roland ... she is liable to be knocked sideways as he erupts into the studio, favouring Garry with a baleful point-blank beam. Conversely, the production also has the confidence to come almost to a dead stop when conversation and action run down, thus preserving the marvellous improvisational sense of this most carefully organized comedy.

Irving Wardle, *The Times*, 4 Apr. 1977

This Happy Breed

Comedy in three acts.
Written: 1939.
First London production: played alternately with *Present Laughter*, Haymarket Th., 30 Apr. 1943 (dir. Coward; des. Gladys Calthrop; with Coward as Frank Gibbons, Joyce Cary as Sylvia, and Judy Campbell as Ethel).
Film version: Cineguild for Two Cities, 1944 (dir. David Lean; prod. Coward).
Published: London: Heinemann, 1943; London: Samuel French, 1945; Garden City, New York: Doubleday, 1947; in *Play Parade, Vol. 4;* and in *Plays: Four.*

There are nine scenes, each of which adds something sad or amusing to our knowledge of the Gibbons family and their neighbours at Clapham Common. The father and the man next door have forged in the war from which they have just returned a bond of harmless conviviality and understanding which is to survive the chances and charges that must be met before the next war looms before them. A daughter and son might so easily parallel this bond, but Queenie Gibbons is a manicurist with a dreadful fear of being as 'common' as her family.... The girl's sudden flight from home is the nodal point of the play's narrative, and it enables Miss Judy Campbell to draw with strength and subtlety the character of a hard-working, loyal wife whose tenacious respectability compels her to be as hard as steel to a daughter who has sinned.

There is a warm-hearted, wholly delightful description of a family wedding as rich in comic characterization as the wedding of Mr. Polly. There is a great deal — perhaps rather too much — of family bickering ... and there is a quite unnecessary motor accident which has no dramatic value and is merely the pretext for a repetitive emotional display. But except for this single lapse Mr. Coward keeps firm control of his narrative and in his own part occasionally permits himself to speak for an England which, though tired, is still possessed of an invincible stamina.

The Times, 1 May 1943

Blithe Spirit

An 'improbable farce' in three acts.
Written: 1941.
First London production: Piccadilly Th., 2 July 1941; trans.
  St. James's Th., 23 Mar. 1942; trans. Duchess Th., 6 Oct. 1942
  (dir. Coward; des. Gladys Calthrop; with Cecil Parker as
  Charles Condomine, Fay Compton as Ruth, Kay Hammond as
  Elvira, and Margaret Rutherford as Madame Arcati).
First New York production: Morosco Th., 5 Nov. 1941.
Revived: Olympia Th., Dublin, 4 Oct. 1954; Globe Th., 23 July
  1970 (dir. Nigel Patrick); National Th., London; 24 June
  1976 (dir. Harold Pinter); Vaudeville Th., 30 Jan. 1986.
Film version: Cineguild, for Two Cities Films, 1945 (dir. David
  Lean).
Published: Garden City, New York: Doubleday, 1941; London:
  Heinemann, 1942; in *Play Parade, Vol. 5;* and in *Plays: Four.*

Mr. Condomine, a novelist in search of copy, invokes Madame Arcati to provide an ectoplasmic evening, and ... Mr. Condomine finds himself with the spectre of his dead wife on his hands as well as with the living reality of his second. ... Elvira Condomine ... is not at all a nice ghost. ... She has returned to be sulkily jealous and to plague her successor. ... Before long [she] becomes as mischievous as a poltergeist and manages to dispose of her living rival. ... However, Mr. Condomine is now a man with a brace of uxorial bogeys. ... His problem, and that of Madame Arcati, is how to make the dear departed actually once more depart ...

The end takes too long to arrive and Mr. Coward's touch deserts him when he makes Mr. Condomine gloat over his new-found freedom from women. The acid here corrodes the honest metal of the previous drollery. The joke may not quite last the three-act distance ... but we can trust Mr. Coward to make both his mortals and immortals cut some capital capers.... Miss Rutherford as Madame Arcati ... presents a gorgeous cartoon of Mind, Matter, and Mumbo-Jumbo. It is she who establishes the piece as riotous nonsense; did it ever slip closer to reality, it might turn to a fatally sour kind of fun.

Ivor Brown, *Punch*, 9 July 1941

Without a single lapse into improbability it achieves the impossible. ... The author's light, easy, amusing way with ectoplasm, poltergeists, hypnotic trances and the like is so adroitly sustained, so much a matter of cause and effect on the comic plane, that we are surprised only as we are meant to be surprised when at the bidding of the briskly fantastic, madly sincere Mme Arcati the first Mrs. Condomine returns after death to make herself scandalously at home in her husband's pleasant Kentish country house. She is a minx, though an engaging minx. Since her departure her husband has married a woman whose sympathetic dignity entitles her to respect. Needless to say, she gets no respect from the minx, and in due course the husband has two disembodied spirits on his hands. So has the dramatist, but he is until the penultimate scene infinitely the less embarrassed of the two.... It is by no means an easy dramatic knot to untie and the dénouement carries the possibly ungallant and certainly facile implication that wives present only one problem to the well-regulated masculine mind: how are they to be got rid of?

The Times, 3 July 1941

Coward's technique in this play is a simple yet effective one: he grafts all the frenzied jealousies and petty deceits of the standard adultery comedy on to a deliciously unlikely story of a novelist plagued by his first wife's ghost. He develops the situation with impeccable logic, places the best lines with his wonted accuracy and also parades all his stylistic trade marks: thus we have the use of deliberately prosaic place names, the jocular references to things revered by the literati (such as psychoanalysts and the BBC music service) and the employment of prime governessy rebuke.

He himself described the piece as an improbably farce and my one reservation about Nigel Patrick's production is that it treats it instead as a believable comedy with too much emphasis on the verbal subtlety and not enough whirlwind pace. It does, however, contain a pair of splendid performances. The more remarkable is Patrick Cargill's as the husband. The character often seems to be a feed for everyone else on stage: Mr. Cargill brilliantly transforms him into an incipient neurotic behind whose bland exterior there lurks a vein of baffled outrage and waspish intensity.

Michael Billington, *The Times*, 24 July 1970

Sigh No More

Revue.
Written: 1945.
First London production: Piccadilly Th., 22 Aug. 1945 ('written, composed, and directed' Coward; des. Gladys Calthrop).
Published: selections in *The Noël Coward Song Book* and *The Lyrics of Noël Coward:* London: Chappell, 1945 (sheet music); book *unpublished.*

Mr. Noël Coward's salute to the Victory mood has ... the humour known of old. ... There are several glances to the Victorian or Edwardian set pieces, thriftily mounted but with the Calthrop touch. ...

The one big episode on quite familiar lines is a burlesque of a Big House pageant; easy for Mr. Coward but very good plain fun it is. As rhymer, the author is in his neatest form ... with excellently worded ditties about the small talk of the Sahib and distaste for the dance in Argentina. Mr. Clifford Gordon has some good minutes of linguistic nonsense, and Miss Joyce Grenfell, supplying some of her own material, is once more, and most decisively, one of our conquerors.

The Observer, 26 Aug. 1945

In February [1945] I went to Tintagel for a week by myself. ... It ... gave me time to assemble some ideas for a revue I was planning for the summer. The planning was then only tentative because although it was generally presumed that the war would end within a few months, this was by no means certain, and if it didn't end I knew that I should have to be up and away again. At all events I had thought of a good title, *Sigh No More,* which later, I regret to say, turned out to be the best part of the revue.

Coward, *Future Indefinite*, p. 330

[See also Coward's *Diaries*, 23 Feb. 1946.]

Pacific 1860

Musical romance.
Written: 1946.
First London production: Theatre Royal, Drury Lane, 19 Dec.
   1946 (dir. Coward; des. Gladys Calthrop; with Mary Martin as
   Elena Salvador and Graham Payn as Kerry Stirling).
Published: London: Chappell, 1947 (vocal score); and
   in *Play Parade, Vol. 5.*

Will anybody deny that the plot of this piece sounds the lowest depths of banality, being all about a prima donna who, as Damon Runyon would have said, takes a number of peeks at a guy living in the South Pacific, who takes a number of peeks back at her? Obviously when a doll and a guy get to taking peeks back and forth at each other, and he is already engaged to be married and she keeps travelling back and forth to keep her concert engagement in Europe, why, there you are indeed. . . .

The dialogue? . . . Through three and a quarter hours I did not hear one scintillating line. The music? Very pleasant and graceful and soothing and accomplished and full of perfunctory lusciousness, but all out of the stock-pot common to purveyors of pseudo-Viennese sentimentalism in waltz-time. . . . About Miss Mary Martin's talent I cannot say more than that she has a nice talking way with her and a tiny voice that would do better in a band-box setting.

James Agate, *Sunday Times*

There is nothing more confusing for actors than play scenes that have been cut or telescoped or transposed. However it can all be achieved with comparative ease during a short provincial tour or a concentrated period of full dress-rehearsals. Poor *Pacific 1860* had neither, and although on the first night it sailed through miraculously well considering, I was fully aware that the kindly audience and the far from kindly critics were seeing a performance that was only half as good as it should have been. The company played beautifully, led by Mary Martin who continued to play the part with gallant unfailing verve at every performance for the rest of the run despite the fact that London froze and the business steadily decreased. . . .

Coward, 'Introduction' to *Play Parade, Vol. 5*

[See also Coward's *Diaries*, 23 Nov. 1946-3 Jan. 1947.]

Peace in Our Time

Play in two acts and eight scenes.
Written: 1946.
First London production: Lyric Th., 22 July 1947 (dir.
  Alan Webb 'under the supervision of Noël Coward'; des.
  Gladys Calthrop; with Bernard Lee as Fred Shattock,
  Beatrice Varley as Nora, Maureen Pryor as Doris, and
  Helen Horsey as Alma Boughton).
Published: London: Heinemann, 1947; Garden City, New York:
  Doubleday, 1948; London: Samuel French, 1949; and in
  Play Parade, Vol 5.

---

*Set entirely in the bar of a London pub, the play traces events in
a Britain under German occupation between the winter of 1940
and the eve of liberation in May 1945 through the lives and
attitudes of the family, staff, and regular customers.*

Mr. Noël Coward's new play is a very spirited affair. . . . There is a
large cast of bartenders, lorry drivers, smartly tweeded and
energetic old ladies up from the country, S.S. men, loving
mothers, Gauleiters, patriotic novelists, and editors of left-wing
weeklies. All these characters are sharply etched. . . . [But] only
once, when a broken and tortured girl is thrown roughly through
the doorway on to the floor of the bar, do the thumbscrews and
whips of [Jean-Paul Sartre's] *Men without Shadows* obtrude
themselves. . . . *Peace in Our Time* misses the horror of occupation. . . . Its sentiments are those of Rudyard Kipling; . . . their
expression unhappily recalls the late G.R. Sims and Adelphi
melodrama.

Harold Hobson, Sunday Times, 27 July 1947

The idea of *Peace in Our Time* was conceived in Paris shortly
after the Liberation. . . . the city itself seemed to be unchanged,
physically at least untouched by the horrors of enemy occupation.
It didn't take me long however to realize that behind the facade
a great deal had changed; the sense of immediate relief had faded
and there was an atmosphere of subtle disintegration, lassitude,
and, above all, suspicion. . . . There was an epidemic of malicious
denunciation, some of it justified, a great deal of it not. . . . This
. . . led me to wonder what might have happened to London and

England if, in 1940, the Germans had successfully invaded and occupied us, which they so very nearly did. . . . I decided to place the entire action in the bar-parlour of a London pub, that being the most easily manageable meeting-ground for various types of Londoners.

Coward, 'Introduction' to *Play Parade, Vol. 5*

[See also Coward's *Diaries*, 3 Nov. 1946, 22 and 23 July 1947.]

South Sea Bubble

Light comedy in three acts, originally *Home and Colonial*, and in US *Island Fling*.

Written: 1949.

First London production: Lyric Th., 25 Apr. 1956 (dir. William Chappell; des. Peter Snow; with Vivien Leigh as Lady Alexandra Shotter, Ronald Lewis as Hali Alani, Alan Webb as Punalo Lewis, Joyce Carey as Cuckoo Honey, and Arthur Macrae as Kennedy).

First American production: Country Playhouse, Westport, Connecticut, 22 July 1951 (dir. John C. Wilson).

Published: London: Heinemann, 2956; and in *Play Parade, Vol 6.*

The main theme concerns the Governor's lady in the Isle of Samolo who plays with native fire, nearly gets her wings singed, bashes her native admirer with a bottle, and at one of those Coward next-morning-at-breakfast scenes slips her way out of the scrape with feline grace.

Manchester Guardian, 27 Apr. 1956

Through [the characters] one sees the father-figure of Mr. Coward, guardian of empire, promoter of the tedious fiction that all coloured people are happy, smiling backward Tories while all British administrators are seedy and frustrated Socialists. The Labour governor of Samolo instructs his wife to wean the reactionary young native leader away from Conservatism; misunderstanding her advances, he reciprocates and has to be whacked over the head with a bottle. . . .

If the message sticks in one's throat, one positively chokes over the dialogue through which he transmits it . . .

The Observer, 29 Apr. 1956

South Sea Bubble . . . was written originally for Gertrude Lawrence . . . and if her tragic death [in 1952] had not intervened she would probably have played it after the end of the run of *The King and I. . . .*

While I am prepared to admit that it does not rank among my best comedies . . . it still has, to my prejudiced eye, a great deal to recommend it. I find 'Sandra' a gay and enchanting character, so much so that I have re-introduced her in my recent novel *Pomp and Circumstance*. 'Hali Alani', 'George Shotter' and 'Cuckoo Honey' have also achieved this literary distinction, although in a minor degree.

To be honest, I consider the first act to be rather verbose and lacking in action, but from then on the play gathers momentum and I have found it highly entertaining both to write and to read.

Coward, 'Introduction' to *Play Parade, Vol 6*

[See also Coward's *Diaries,* 6 Apr. and 3 May 1949, 27 June 1950, 10 and 14 Mar. 1955, and 20 May 1956.]

Ace of Clubs

Musical play in two acts.
Written: 1949.
First London production: Cambridge Th., 7 July 1950 (dir. Coward; des. Gladys Calthrop; with Pat Kirkwood as Pinkie Leroy and Graham Payn as Harry Hornby).
Published: in *Play Parade, Vol. 6;* selections in *The Lyrics of Noël Coward;* London: Chappell, 1950.

The story of an honest sailor who falls in and out of the hands of gangsters as a consequence of trying to protect the night club singer he loves.

The stage diversions on the floor of the night club usefully punctuate, but give little other help to, the action. There is some gentle satire, but, for the most part, they are all too like the kind of floor show that we imagine might be found in a second-rate Soho night club. The decorations are the best things of the evening — the three juvenile delinquents, who are as happy as can be with the 'coshes' in their pockets and a sure faith in psycho-analysis and judges who will duly hand them over to the probation officer. . . . These unfortunately are called on for a second time to bolster the weaker, second half of the show, and do not warrant quite so much confidence.

The Times, 8 July 1950

Ace of Clubs was another attempt to break away from a tradition I had established for myself. With the exception of revues my only 'musicals' to date had been in period — *Bitter-Sweet* Victorian, *Conversation Piece* Regency, *Operette* Edwardian, and *Pacific 1860* Victorian Colonial. I considered that the time had come to write a musical play in a modern setting with contemporary songs. Most of the contemporary songs were good but the book was uninspired and was not helped by either the setting or the production. . . . After a triumphant opening in Manchester . . . it subsequently opened at the Cambridge Theatre . . . and pottered along for 211 performances. There is not much more to be said about it really. . . . At least it anticipated the present rash of Soho-Gangster British musicals by some years, so I can always comfort myself with the reflection that it was 'Before its Time'.

Coward, 'Introduction' to *Play Parade, Vol. 6*

[See also Coward's *Diaries*, 27 Dec. 1949, 12 Jan., 18 Feb., and 8 July, 1950].

Relative Values

Light comedy in three acts.
Written: 1951.
First London production: Savoy Th., 28 Nov. 1951 (dir. Coward; des. Michael Relph; with Angela Baddeley as Mrs. Moxton, Gladys Cooper as the Countess of Marshwood, Ralph Michael as Nigel, Richard Leech as Crestwell, and Judy Campbell as Miranda).
First American production: Arena Th. Rochester, N.J., 24 Mar. 1954.

Revived: Westminster Th., 6 Sept. 1973.
Published: London: Heinemann, 1952; in *Play Parade, Vol. 5;*
  and in *Plays: Five.*

---

*A mellow dowager countess . . . thinks it 'quite beastly' when her
son gets himself tied up with a painted film hussy named Miranda
Frayle. She sets out to smash the romance. Her nice humble
maid, Moxie, is even more shocked. For Miranda is revealed as
Moxie's long-lost sister – and a brat. To save her maid from feeling
inferior, the countess dresses up Moxie in grand clothes and
spectacles. She introduces her to Miranda as a friend of the family.
Miranda does not even recognize her. She is too busy patronizing
her hosts. It is too much for Moxie, who tears off her specs and
denounces her sister as the disgrace of a respectable family. After
that it is easy for the countess with her calculated poise to
embarrass and insult the nasty intruder out of her house.*

John Barber, *Daily Express,* 29 Nov. 1951

His doctrine, if you seek it, is a simple contempt for current
dogma about equality; but his purpose is light comedy, not heavy
polemic. His social landscape is strangely untouched by the Age
of Anxiety. . . . The family mansion has not passed to the
National Trust . . . there is still a butler and a feminine staff. He is
a fine period piece, this butler, not a sly and slangy Jeeves, but
one who mingles occasional epigram with the vocabulary of a
Gladstone. The servants open his play by explaining the situation,
a device not unknown to dramatists since drawing-room began. . . .
There is a sensible break with tradition in showing us the 'drunk',
not as a chattering, swaggering, guffawing ass, but as a stuffed
owl, glassy-eyed and walking with the stiffness born of a desperate
determination to pass as sober. This is delicious comedy.

  Angela Baddeley, as the star's humble sister . . . does not put a
move or intonation wrong. The second act, following an occasionally sluggish first, is very much hers. . . . The dramatist has left
the players with an empty third act, which vaccum they easily
conceal.

Ivor Brown, *The Observer,* 2 Dec. 1951

Quadrille

Romantic comedy in three acts.
Written: 1951-52.
First London production: Phoenix Th., 12 Sept. 1952 (dir.
    Coward; des. Cecil Beaton; with Lynn Fontanne as Serena,
    Alfred Lunt as Axel Diensen, Joyce Carey as Lady Harriet,
    and Griffith Jones as Herbert).
First American production: Cornet Th., New York, 3 Nov. 1954
    (dir. Alfred Lunt; with Lynne Fontanne and Alfred Lunt).
Published: London: Heinemann, 1952; London: Samuel French,
    1954; Garden City, New York: Doubleday, 1955; and in
    Play Parade, Vol. 5.

*We first meet the Marquess of Heronden running away to the
Riviera with the wife of an American railroad magnate; he is a gay
blade . . . and she a brisk Bostonian. Presently the Marchioness
and the tycoon pursue their spouses and succeed in reclaiming
them by sheer force of argument. It is now the end of Act Two
and the plot . . . hereafter . . . thins rather than thickens. Milady
and the magnate discover that they, too, are in love, and the play
ends where it began, in the station buffet at Boulogne en route
for the Mediterranean. . . .*

Miss Fontanne plays the madcap Marchioness with the crackle
and sheen of a five pound note. Her eyes mock marvellously, her
voice cuts like a knife into a wedding cake, and the scene in Act
Three, on the eve of her elopement with Mr. Lunt, is as delicious
as crushed ice. Given one sprig of wit to adorn it, this would have
been a gorgeous bouquet; but, alas, everything is said twice over,
and what was meant for a gracious sparkle ends up as a con-
descending wink.

Mr. Lunt, who is not intended to be witty, accordingly makes
much more of the clumsy, artless millionaire. Bearded and brush-
cropped, with plaintive eyes, he looks like a Greek god turned
beachcomber, and his voice has the texture of gnarled oak. But
charm and technique, however loving, are not proof against over-
writing. . . . Under the weight of the lines, the plot collapses, and
we are left only with negative virtues.

The play is not snobbish, it is not vulgar, nor is it without
style; but it is also not the pure fantastic Coward at whose
invention we used to chuckle long after the curtain had dropped.

Kenneth Tynan, *Evening Standard,* 13 Sept. 1952

Quadrille, which I wrote specifically for Lynn Fontanne and Alfred Lunt, is a romantic Victorian comedy which the critics detested and the public liked enough to fill the Phoenix Theatre for a year. It has, to my biased mind, a great deal to recommend it. To enlarge on the Lunts' performance of it would be redundant. . . . In addition to their ineffable contribution, the décor and the dresses were designed with exquisite colour and taste by Cecil Beaton. In addition even to these matchless attributes it has in it some evocative and well written scenes, notably the 'Railway' speech spoken by . . . 'Axel' in Act Three, Scene Three.

Later on I saw an excellent performance of *Quadrille* at the Connaught Theatre, Worthing, without the Lunts or the Beaton décor, and believe it or not the much abused little piece stood up remarkably well.

Coward, 'Introduction' to *Play Parade, Vol. 5*

[See also Coward's *Diaries,* 13-19 Sept. 1952.]

After the Ball

Musical play, based on Oscar Wilde's *Lady Windermere's Fan.*
Written: 1953.
First London production: Globe Th., 10 June 1954 (dir. Robert Helpmann; des. Doris Zinkeisen; with Vanessa Lee as Lady Windermere, Peter Graves as Lord Windermere, Mary Ellis as Mrs Erlynne, Graham Payn as Mr. Hopper, Irene Browne as the Duchess, and Patricia Cree as Lady Agatha).
First American production: Terrell's Music Circus, Lambertville, N.J., 2 Aug. 1955.
Published: London: Chappell, 1954 (score); and selections in *The Lyrics of Noël Coward;* book *unpublished.*

It was by no means easy for the first-night audience to get the proper hang of the thing. . . . They were misled by the opening scene. Here were the ladies of the nineties . . . parading in the park and crying out to each other with a lively consciousness of their place in history, 'Oh, what a century it has been!' . . . But no sooner had we got ready to enjoy a burlesque than we found Mr. Coward plunging into the story of the play. We heard Lord and Lady Windermere singing a song of perfect conjugal felicity,

Lord Darlington hinting at his love for Lady Windermere and receiving no encouragement from the lady, and the Duchess of Berwick confiding with gay irresponsibility in Windermere's wife that Windermere's liaison with the notorious Mrs Erlynne had now become the talk of the town. . . .

The shattering of the Windermere idyll made a good curtain, with poor Lady Windermere singing now with infinite sadness of that 'sweet day' which but a little ago she was extolling with rapture. But the audience by this time hardly knew whether they were supposed to be laughing at Wilde or Victorianism. . . . It was only the final scene which made the audience realize that the whole thing should have taken in the spirit of musical comedy . . . and the applause at the final curtain was a sort of retrospective recognition that lurking amidst the confusion there had been many enjoyable things.

Anthony Cookman, *The Tatler*, 23 June 1954

[See also Coward's *Diaries*, 1 and 21 Apr., 13 June 1955.]

Nude with Violin

Light comedy in three acts.
Written: 1954.
First London production: Globe Th., 7 Nov. 1956 (dir. John Gielgud and Coward; des. Paul Anstee; with Gielgud as Sebastien, Patience Collier as Anya Pavlikov, Kathleen Harrison as Cherry-May Waterton, and Joyce Carey as Isobel Sorodin).
First American production: Belasco Th., New York, 14 Nov. 1957.
Published: in *Plays and Players*, Dec. 1956 and Jan. 1957; London: Heinemann, 1957; London and New York: Samuel French, 1958; and in *Play Parade, Vol. 6*.

Gathering after the funeral of a famous artist, his family and agent learn that his entire output was fraudulent, and eventually submit to a blackmail which sustains both the myth and the market value of the paintings.

The author who could [once] whip off a rollickingly funny line, catch a fleeting mood, sketch in a comedy with a few swift strokes, has dwindled into a mere playmaker who can still hold the stage but whose dialogue all too rarely achieves those little shocks of surprise which make all the difference. . . .

[The play] has one entirely successful scene. . . . The dead man's confidential valet . . . chooses exactly the right moment to read a letter from the great Sorodin saying that he has cheerfully spent all the money he earned and confessing with blatant satisfaction that his masterpieces were without exception painted by other hands. Mr. Coward works up to this disclosure with all his old impudent dexterity, and the artful valet manages it delightfully. . . . [This] disclosure leaves his most interesting character a corpse; and the rest of his play depends on a slow parade of hirelings who painted the masterpieces.

Anthony Cookman, *Tatler and Bystander,* 21 Nov. 1956

Nude with Violin is a satirical light comedy which received almost unanimous abuse from the critics and ran to capacity for eighteen months. . . .

My personal opinion of it is that although it achieved its original purpose, which was to entertain the public and at the same time satirize certain aspects of 'Modern Art Appreciation', it did not completely succeed because the situation of the play as established at the end of the first act becomes a trifle threadbare by the end of the last. I was acutely aware of this structural defect when I way playing the part of 'Sebastien' myself, much more so than when I wrote it. The critics pounced on this failing with ill-concealed satisfaction and of course they were quite right to do so. They were not quite right however to dismiss the play as a whole with withering contempt. It has in it some excellent character drawing and some fine comedy scenes.

Coward, 'Introduction' to *Play Parade, Vol. 6*

Look after Lulu!

Adaptation of Feydeau's *Occupe-toi d'Amélie.*
Written: 1958.
First London production: English Stage Company, Royal Court Th., 29 July 1959; trans. New Th., 8 Sept. 1959 (dir. Tony Richardson; with Vivien Leigh as Lulu, Anthony Quayle as Marcel Blanchard, George Devine as Herr van Poutzebum, and Max Adrian as the Prince of Salestria).
First American production: Henry Miller's Th., New York, 3 Mar 1959.

Look after Lulu!

Revived: Chichester Festival Th., 26 July 1978; trans. Haymarket
   Th., 9 Oct. 1978 (dir. Patrick Garland; with Geraldine McEwan
   as Lulu, Clive Francis as Marcel, and Peter Bowles as the Prince).
Published: London: Heinemann, 1959; and in *Plays: Five*.

*Lulu of the title is an attractive little tart, mistress of every situation
and of every man she has an eye to. Philippe, her truest love, off
to do his army service, entrusts her to his best friend, Marcel. He,
Marcel, does not love her particularly, but wants her to go
through a mock marriage ceremony with him so that he can come
into a fortune. Lulu, always ready to oblige, consents to be looked
after and mock-married, while making her own arrangements
about a rich and generous Oriental prince. The various plans
collide, miscarry, collapse, and revive in the most bewildering
fashion and finally arrive at an equilibrium of sorts.*

W.A. Darlington, *Daily Telegraph,* 30 July 1950

Noël Coward's adaptation of Feydeau's *Occupe-toi d'Amelie* had
the bad luck to be caught in the crossfire of the radical theatre
campaign when the Royal Court staged it in 1959. Brought in as a
sure-fire West End hit to keep the Court in business, it failed to
do the trick and became a byword among experimental companies
on the folly of selling out for fairy gold. All of which was most
unfair to Coward, who was only guilty of adapting Feydeau for
Britain some years before the arrival of the Feydeau boom.
French farce at that time was considered unplayable by English
actors. What they could play was high comedy with plenty of
vocal pirouettes. Accordingly, Coward made his version, inserting,
as his collaborator Cole Lesley says, 'too many Coward jokes for
Feydeau's good'. I only wish there had been more jokes and that
Coward had entirely transformed the play instead of merely
tinkering with it.

Irving Wardle, *The Times,* 26 July 1978

[See also Coward's *Diaries,*   22 June 1958, 11 Mar., 5 Apr., and
   2 Aug. 1959]

London Morning

Ballet.
Written: 1958-59.
First London production: London Festival Ballet Company,
    Festival Hall, 14 July 1959, in repertoire for three years (score
    by Noël Coward; chor. Jack Carter; des. William Constable;
    costumes Norman McDowell.)

Anyone who tries to approach *London Morning* as a ballet is
doomed to disappointment. . . . *London Morning* is much more
accurately revue dance-sketches which are to be seen in variety
shows or on television. It shows a succession of varied characters
passing outside Buckingham Palace, schoolgirls, teddy-boys, ladies
of easy virtue, nuns, a spiv and his family, an old man in his bath-
chair, and others. The atmosphere is frankly artificial and it is out
of date too — so is the music, much of which would not have
seemed *avant-garde* if Sullivan had penned it in the reign of our
previous queen. Judged on its own terms, which are not those of
ballet, it is gay and effective enough.

The Times, 15 July, 1959

[See also Coward's *Diaries*, 7 Sept., 5 Oct. 1958, and 19 July
    1959.]

Waiting in the Wings

Play in three acts.
Written: 1959-60.
First London production: Duke of York's Th., 7 Sept. 1960
    (dir. Margaret Webster; with Marie Lohr as May Davenport and
    Sybil Thorndike as Lotta Bainbridge).
Published: London: Heinemann, 1960; Garden City, New York:
    Doubleday, 1960; London and New York; Samuel French,
    1960; in *Play Parade, Vol. 6;* and in *Play: Five.*

*The subject of Mr. Coward's new play is a charity home for
retired actresses. . . . There are the two old actresses who haven't
spoken for thirty years and at last make it up. There is Christmas
night in the orphanage, and the case of champagne sent in by a*

*well-wisher. There is the poor old girl who is off her head and
thinks she is still on tour and is always delivering lines from one
of her plays. There is the tough old Irish actress who ups and
dances a jig, and collapses dead in front of us. There is even . . . the
prodigal son returning after thirty years neglect to take Mother
away from the shame of charity – and being bravely rejected.*

There is a lot of old shop talked and a lot of old songs sung, and
it gets more nauseating . . . as the evening wears on.

T.C. Worsley, *Financial Times*, 8 Sept. 1960

Probably the play will . . . serve as a broad target for scorn in some
quarters, and may justifiably be called shameless in its exploitation
of the sentimentalities inherent in a tale of old actresses backbiting
and sighing in a home for the aged of the profession. . . . But as
long as the mood is one of outraged grandeur, mild dottiness,
theatrical slander, and the game of up-staging the last speaker,
Mr. Coward's touch remains what it has always been: and
sometimes touches the level of inspired cattiness found in such
pieces as *The Red Peppers.* . . .

Philip Hope Wallace, *Manchester Guardian,* 9 Sept. 1960

My own personal opinion of the play is biased by my deep
affection for it. . . . I wrote *Waiting in the Wings* with loving care
and absolute belief in its characters. I consider that the reconciliation between 'Lotta' and 'May' in Act Two, Scene Three, and
the meeting of 'Lotta' and her son in Act Three, Scene Two, are
two of the best scenes I have ever written. I consider that the play
as a whole contains, beneath the froth of some of its lighter
moments, the basic truth that old age needn't be nearly so dreary
and sad as it is supposed to be, provided you greet it with humour
and live it with courage.

Coward, 'Introduction' to *Play Parade, Vol. 6*

[See also Coward's *Diaries,* 1 May 1958, 22 Apr., 15 Aug., 11
Sept. 1960, and 7 Jan. 1961.]

Sail Away

Musical comedy.
Written: 1959-61.
First London production: Savoy Th., 21 June 1962 (dir. Coward; des. Loudon Sainthill; with Elaine Stritch as Mimi, David Holliday as Johnny van Mier, Mavis Villiers as Mrs. Van Mier, and Grover Dale as Barnaby Slade).
First American production: Broadhurst Th., New York, 3 Oct. 1961 (dir. Coward).
Published: selections in *The Lyrics of Noël Coward;* book *unpublished.*

Mr. Coward's... dramatis personae *are passengers, all but two American, on a sunny cruise, and the show's centre is the ship's social hostess.... There are two love affairs: that of Sheila Forbes's delicious feather-brained teenager for Mr. Grover Dale's would-be archeologist... is lively and gently funny,... but the love of young Johnny van Mier for Miss Elaine Stritch's hostess... does not run smooth.*

The Times, 22 June 1962

Basically, its a good old-fashioned musical: colour scenes, and comedy scenes, backdrops of Tangier and the Pantheon, travel jokes, American jokes, and smutty jokes, and a clutch of shipboard romances.... But open the bright wrappings and what's inside? In the first half the answer is not very much.... Mr. Coward takes an unconscionable time in getting his American to Europe, and the bon-bons were few and far between.

After the interval, the transformation. The drops of acid, so long awaited, suddenly appeared, so did one or two of those mercurial lyrics which seem to create their own music.

If the old nostalgia looks a little shop-soiled in places and the romance is sometimes palely middle-aged, then one must be indulgent. The second act of *Sail Away* offers just about the most enjoyable hour to be found in the West End at the moment.

John Higgins, *Financial Times,* 22 June 1962

[See also Coward's *Diaries,* 26 Oct. 1958, 29 Oct. 1961, and 2 July 1961.]

Suite in Three Keys

Trilogy comprising *A Song at Twilight*, 'a comedy in two acts';
   Shadows of the Evening 'a play in two scenes'; and *Come into*
   the Garden Maud, 'a light comedy in one act and two scenes'.
Written: 1965.
First London production: Queen's Th., in repertoire, 14 and 25
   Apr. 1966 (dir. Vivian Matelon; with Seän Barrett, Noël
   Coward, Lilli Palmer, and Irene Worth).
First New York production: as *Noël Coward in Two Keys*
   comprising *Come into the Garden Maud* and *A Song at*
   Twilight, Ethel Barrymore Th., 28 Feb. 1974 (dir. Vivian
   Matelon).
Published: London: Heinemann, 1966; Garden City, New York:
   Doubleday, 1967; London: Samuel French, 1967 (separate
   editions of each title); and in *Plays: Five*.

For all their determined glitter and the authentic disclaimers of any purpose beyond entertainment, Noël Coward's plays are among the most earnestly moral works to be found anywhere in modern drama; and in *A Song at Twilight* ... he slips off all comic disguise and returns to the vein of melodramatic indignation with which, in plays like *Fumed Oak* and *The Vortex*, he began his career. ... It seems, beyond question, to be based on the last years of Somerset Maugham — its central figure being a celebrated old writer who has managed to conceal his weaknesses from the world at the price of warping his talent and cutting off his human sympathies. The title refers to Goethe's warning against self-denial.

The form ... is that of the old-fashioned problem play in which an eminent public figure is visited by an old acquaintance who possesses scandalous information about the past. In this case, the visitor is an ex-mistress with whom Hugh Latymer had once attempted to acquire hetrosexual taste: now she returns bearing love letters he had written to his male secretary which also show him in the act of cold-hearted betrayal. ...

This formula permits Mr. Coward to address a strong plea for homosexual tolerance to a popular West End audience; and to anatomize with painful accuracy the effect of emotional withdrawal on his hermit-crab hero.

The Times, 15 Apr. 1966

a: Screenplays

In Which We Serve
Two Cities Films, 1942 (dir. Coward and David Lean,
  with Coward, John Mills, and Bernard Miles). [Based
  on the sinking of HMS Kelly and still considered a
  masterpiece of wartime propaganda. For an account
  of planning and production, see *Future Indefinite.*]

Brief Encounter
(Still Life from *To-Night at 8.30).* Cineguild, 1945
  (script in *Three British Screenplays,* ed. Roger Manvell.
  London: Methuen, 1950).

The Astonished Heart
Gainsborough Films, 1949-50 (with incidental music by
  Coward).

b: Lyrics

Collected Sketches and Lyrics
with introduction by Coward. London: Hutchinson,
  1931.

The Noël Coward Song Book
with introduction and annotations by Coward. London:
  Joseph, 1953.

The Lyrics of Noël Coward
with introduction by Coward. London: Heinemann, 1965.

c: Novel

Pomp and Circumstance
London: Heinemann, 1960; Methuen, 1983. [The
  inhabitants of Samolo — previously featured in *South
  Sea Bubble* — are 'all in rather a frizz' as they prepare
  for the arrival of the Queen. Also come to stay is the
  flighty Duchess of Fowey, to pursue her adulterous
  affair with Bunny.]

d: Short Stories

To Step Aside
London: Heinemann, 1939. [Seven short stories.]

Star Quality
London: Heinemann, 1951.

Pretty Polly Barlow, and Other Stories
London: Heinemann, 1964; Mayflower Books, 1964.

Bon Voyage and Other Stories
London: Heinemann, 1967.

Collected Short Stories
introduced by the author and selected by him, from *To Step Aside* and *Star Quality*. London: Heinemann, 1962; Methuen, 1983, in two volumes, and in one volume as *The Complete Stories*, 1985.

e: Verse and Parodies

A Withered Nosegay
imaginary biographies, with reproductions from old masters by Lorn Macnaughton. London: Christophers, 1922. Revised, as *Terribly Intimate Portraits*, New York: Boni and Liveright, 1922.

Chelsea Buns
by Hernia Whittlebot, edited by Noël Coward with introduction by Gaspard Pustontin. London: Hutchinson, 1925. [Parodies of the Sitwells.]

Spangled Unicorn
a selection from the works of Albrecht Drausler, Serge Sliavonov, Janet Urdler, etc. London: Hutchinson, 1932.

Not Yet the Dodo, and Other Verses
London: Heinemann, 1967.

A Withered Nosegay: Three Cod Pieces
[Includes *A Withered Nosegay*, *Chelsea Buns*, and *A Spangled
    Unicorn*] London: Methuen 1984.

Collected Verse
ed. Graham Payn and Martin Tickner. London: Methuen, 1984.

f: Autobiography and Diaries

Present Indicative
London: Heinemann, 1937, 1974. [Childhood years, and career
    to 1931.]

Future Indefinite
London: Heinemann, 1954; New York: Doubleday, 1954;
    Da Capo Press, 1980. [Covers the years 1939-1946.]

Autobiography
with an introduction by Sheridan Morley. London: Methuen,
    1986. [Includes both the above titles, and the uncompleted
    Past Conditional, covering 1931-1939.]

The Noël Coward Diaries
ed. Graham Payn and Sheridan Morely. London: Weidenfeld
    and Nicholson, 1982 [Cover the last thirty years of his life.]

Australia Visited
London: Heinemann, 1941. [Reprinted wartime broadcasts.]

Middle East Diary
London; Toronto: Heinemann, 1944. [July to October 1943.]

The process of writing

I can see no particular virtue in writing quickly; on the contrary, I am well aware that too great a facility is often dangerous, and should be curbed when it shows signs of getting the bit too firmly between its teeth. No reputable writer should permit his talent to bolt with him. I am also aware though, from past experience, that when the right note is struck and the structure of a play is carefully built in advance, it is both wise and profitable to start at the beginning and write through to the end in as short a time as possible. . .

Before the first word of the first act is written, the last act should be clearly in the author's mind, if not actually written out in the form of a synopsis. Dialogue, for those who have a talent for it, is easy; but construction, with or without talent, is difficult and is of paramount importance. . . .

Future Indefinite, 1954

On the importance of comedy

Deeply embedded in most people's minds is the conviction that a work of art can only merit the adjective 'important' if it deals with a serious matter in a serious manner. Since the grey dawn of the Christian era this superstition has persisted, presumably because laughter, frivolity, joy, and humour are concomitants of pleasure and for those who accept the dubious assumption that the brief years we live on this earth are merely a preparation for a nobler life to come, pleasure is obviously suspect. . . . Personally I have never been able to share this wary attitude towards enjoyment. I prefer comedy to tragedy and laughter to tears. . . .

It must not be imagined, however, that in my early years I was not beset by doubts. Inspired by my facility for light dialogue and my ingrained appreciation of the more comic aspects of life, I worked away at my comedies and revues and lyrics; they were produced; they were, mostly, successful . . . but all the time, in my deep Christian subconscious, there was the gnawing suspicion that I was nothing but a jester, a foolish, superficial, capering lightweight with neither depths nor real human understanding; that immediately after my death, if not a long while before, my name would be obliterated if not a long while before, my name would be obliterated from public memory.

I searched my mind, for long years I searched, to find a theme solemn enough on which to base a really important play. It was only a little while ago, when I was cheerfully emerging from my forties into my fifties, that, to quote Madame Arcati, 'It came upon me in a blinding flash' that I had already written several important plays — *Hay Fever, Private Lifes, Design for Living. Present Laughter,* and *Blithe Spirit.* These plays were important because they had given a vast number of people a great deal of pleasure.

'Introduction' to *Play Parade, Vol. 5,* 1958

On comic writing and acting

One audience may be good and the next dull. You have to play them like fish, just to get their attention. It's much more fascinating and far, far more difficult than playing a strong emotional part. The emotion carries you through, whereas in a well-written comedy you've got to keep yourself in check. . . . If the dialogue is good, let the dialogue speak. Don't wink. Don't make faces. Don't try to make it funny. . . .

Interview with Hugh Curnow, 1966

Different kinds of success

It is very difficult for me to assess what have been my greatest successes as a writer but, from the point of view of amusement-value and technical craftsmanship, I would select *Blithe Spirit.* The two worst plays I ever wrote were called *Home Chat* and *This Was a Man.* But to describe the work of a writer of my versatility in terms of best or worst is really impossible, I think, and useless to try.

Brief Encounter was one of the most human and touching plays I wrote, whereas *Private Lives* and *Present Laughter* were two of the wittiest. The thing I like best about *Brief Encounter* is that the love scene is played *against* the words. . . . He's a doctor and he talks about preventive medicine and the different diseases one gets, and all the time he's looking at her. And then she says, 'You suddenly look much younger' — which cuts right through and forces them back to ordinary dialogue.

Interview with Hugh Curnow, 1966

On his own musicals

I was born into a generation that took light music seriously. It was fortunate for me that I was, because by the time I had emerged form my teens the taste of the era had changed. In my early twenties and thirties it was from America that I gained my greatest impetus. In New York they have always taken light music seriously. There it is, as it should be, saluted as a specialized form of creative art, and is secure in its own right. The basis of a successful American musical show is now and has been for many years its music and its lyrics. Here in England there are few to write the music and fewer still to recognize it when it is written. . . .

I have, within the last twenty-five years, composed many successful songs and three integrated scores of which I am genuinely proud. These are *Bitter-Sweet, Conversation Piece,* and *Pacific 1860. This Year of Grace* and *Words and Music*, although revues, were also well constructed musically. *Operette* was sadly meagre with the exception of three numbers, 'Dearest Love', 'Where Are the Songs We Sung' and 'The Stately Homes of England'. This latter, however, being a comedy quartet, relied for its success more on its lyrics than its tune.

Ace of Clubs contained several good songs, but could not fairly be described as a musical score. *Sigh No More, On with the Dance,* and *London Calling* are outside this discussion as they were revues containing contributions from other composers. *Bitter-Sweet,* the most flamboyantly successful of all my musical shows, had a full and varied score greatly enhanced by the orchestrations of Orrelana. *Conversation Piece* was less full and varied but had considerable quality. . . .

Pacific 1860 was, musically, my best work to date. It was carefully balanced and well constructed and imaginatively orchestrated by Ronald Binge and Mantovani. The show, as a whole, was a failure. It had been planned on a small scale, but, owing to theatre exigencies and other circumstances, had to be blown up to fit the stage of Drury Lane. . . .

I have often been irritated in later years by my inability to write music down effectively and by my complete lack of knowledge of orchestration except by ear, but being talented from the very beginning in several different media, I was faced by common sense to make a decision. The decision I made was to try to become a good writer and actor, and to compose tunes and harmonies whenever the urge to do so became too powerful to resist.

'Light Music Seriously', *Punch*, 15 and 22 July 1953

The art of revue

The art of revue writing is acknowledged by those unfortunates who have had anything to do with it as being a very tricky and technical business. Everything has to be condensed to an appalling brevity. The biggest laugh must be on the last line before the black out. No scene or number should play for more than a few minutes at most, and, above all, the audience must never be kept waiting. . . .

The lessons which have to be learned by aspiring revue writers are many and bitter. The bitterest really being the eternal bugbear of 'running order' . . . and, however carefully the author may have planned it originally, this sequence is generally completely changed by the time the show reaches dress rehearsal. . . . Another problem . . . is the successful handling of danger spots. The principal danger spots in Revue are (1) The opening of the whole show, which must be original and extremely snappy. (2) The sketch immediately following it, which must so convulse the audience that they are warmed up enough to overlook a few slightly weaker items. (3) The finale of the first half. This should essentially be the high spot of the evening so that on the first night the bulk of the audience and the critics can retire to the bars (if not already there) and, glowing with enthusiasm, can drink themselves into an alcoholic stupor for the second half. The fourth danger spot is the strong low-comedy scene, which should be placed as near as possible to the second-half finale and should be strong, low, and very comic indeed.

'Preface' to *Collected Sketches and Lyrics*, 1931

On actors and techniques of acting

Theatrically, one of the more depressing aspects of the present transitional phase through which the civilized world is passing is the monotonous emphasis on the lot of the Common Man; for the Common Man, unless written and portrayed with genius, is not, dramatically, nearly so interesting as he is claimed to be. . . .

This brings me with a slight yawn to what is colloquially known as the Method. . . . It stresses a few essential 'musts', such as the necessity of finding the correct psychological values of the part to be played and concentrating first on the interior truth of a character before attempting the exterior projection of it. As this, however, is what every experienced actor I have ever met does automatically, I cannot welcome it as a dazzling revelation.

In my opinion the Method places too much emphasis on actual realism and too little on simulated realism. . . . Every intelligent actor realizes the impossibility of *genuinely* feeling the emotions necessary to his part for eight performances a week over a period of months or even years. His art lies in his ability to re-create nightly an accurate simulation of the emotions he originally felt when he was first studying and rehearsing it. . . .

Technique, although a much despised word nowadays, is, beyond a shadow of a doubt, indispensable. . . . It is palpably foolish for an actor to try to play a major role, or even minor ones . . . without first learning to move about the stage and speak audibly. . . .

Another, to my mind, dangerous assumption on the part of the Method teachers is that actors are cerebral and can be relied upon to approach the playing of a part intellectually. In my experience, the really fine actors . . . have been, in varying degrees, intelligent, shrewd, egotistical, temperamental, emotional and above all, intuitive, but never either logical or intellectual. Their approach to their work, according to their respective characters and techniques, is guided almost mystically by their talent. . . . And it is this, curiously enough, in which most of them have the least confidence and for which they require the most reassurance . . . this basic uncertainty is their most valuable and endearing asset. It is also the hall-mark of the genuine article. . . .

Alas and alack, I have encountered quite a number of our young actors and actresses of today who, sodden with pretentious theories and trained to concentrate solely on their own reactions and motivations to the exclusion of their fellow actors and the audience, have not even a bowing acquaintance with humility. . . . They arrogantly condemn the 'commercial' theatre, which in essence means the public that they must ultimately hope to please. . . .

The theatre is a wonderful place, a house of strange enchantment, a temple of illusion. What it most emphatically is not and never will be is a scruffy, ill-lit, fumed-oak drill-hall serving as a temporary soap-box for political propaganda.

'The Scratch-and-Mumble School', *Sunday Times,* 22 Jan. 1961

A critique of the 'new movement.'
In the last decade I have been a fairly detached spectator of what is described as 'The New Movement In The Theatre', and I feel that now, after fifty years of activity in the profession . . . my age and experience entitle me to offer a little gentle advice to the young revolutionaries of today. . . .

My advice, in essence, is simple and can be stated in three words:

Consider the Public. . . . To batter it with propaganda, bewilder it with political ideologies, bore it with class prejudice, and, above all, irritate it with wilful technical inefficiency, is a policy that can only end in dismal frustration and certain failure. . . .

I am a staunch upholder of the theory that a beginner should first write about the class he knows best, but I also believe that, having done so, once or twice or even three times, his allegiance to his own creative talent should compel him to start learning about other classes as soon as he possibly can. It is as dull to write incessantly about tramps and prostitutes as it is to write incessantly about dukes and duchesses or even suburban maters and paters, and it is bigoted and stupid to believe that tramps and prostitutes and underprivileged housewives frying onions and using ironing boards are automatically the salt of the earth. . . .

Equally bigoted is the assumption that reasonably educated people who behave with restraint in emotional crises are necessarily 'clipped', 'arid', 'bloodless', and 'unreal'.

It is true that a writer should try to hold the mirror up to nature, although there are certain aspects of nature which would be better unreflected. In some of the recent 'New Movement' plays I have noted several examples of trivial and entirely unnecessary vulgarity. . . .

It is interesting to note that at the moment of writing there is only one 'New Movement' straight play playing to good business . . . *The Caretaker* by Harold Pinter. . . . Mr. Pinter is neither pretentious, pseudo-intellectual, nor self-consciously propagandist. True, the play has no apparent plot, much of it is repetitious and obscure; but it is written with an unmistakable sense of theatre and is impeccably acted and directed. Above all, its basic premise is victory rather than defeat. . . .

It is well known that there are all sorts of audiences for all sorts of plays. The public that packs the theatre nightly for *Simple Spymen* or *Watch It, Sailor!* is entirely different from that which queues up for *Ross* or Shakespeare seasons at Stratford or the Old Vic. Somehow or other there always seems to be enough to go round. I disagree . . . that the younger playwrights need a 'new' audience. What they need is just an audience, new or old . . . and this, with one or two exceptions, they have so far been unable to get.

'These Old-Fashioned Revolutionaries', *Sunday Times*, 15 Jan. 1961

a: Primary Sources

Collections of Plays
cited elsewhere by short titles, as below

Play Parade. London: Heinemann, 1934-62, in six
volumes.
Vol. 1, 1934: *Cavalcade; Bitter-Sweet; The Vortex;
Hay Fever; Design for Living; Private Lives; Post-
Mortem.*
Vol. 2, 1939: *This Year of Grace; Words and Music;
Operette; Conversation Piece.* Enlarged ed. of 1950
also includes *Easy Virtue* and *Fallen Angels.*
Vol. 3, 1950: *The Queen Was in the Parlour; I'll Leave
It to You; The Young Idea; Sirocco; The Rat Trap;
This Was a Man; Home Chat; The Marquise.*
Vol. 4, 1954: *To-Night at 8.30; Present Laughter;
This Happy Breed.*
Vol. 5, 1958: *Blithe Spirit; Peace in Our Time;
Quadrille; Relative Values; Pacific 1860.*
Vol. 6, 1962: *Point Valaine; South Sea Bubble; Ace
of Clubs; Nude with Violin; Waiting in the Wings.*
Coward: Plays. London: Methuen, 1979-83, in five volumes
(the Master Playwrights' series).
Plays: One, 1979: *Hay Fever; The Vortex; Fallen
Angels; Easy Virtue.*
Plays: Two, 1979: *Private Lives; Bitter-Sweet; The
Marquise; Post-Mortem.*
Plays: Three, 1979: *Design for Living; Cavalcade;
Conversation Piece;* three plays from *To-Night at
8.30.*
Plays: Four, 1979: *Blithe Spirit; Present Laughter;
This Happy Breed;* three plays from *To-Night at
8.30.*
Plays: Five, 1983: *Relative Values; Look after Lulu;
Waiting in the Wings; Suite in Three Keys.*
Three Plays (The Rat Trap, The Vortex, Fallen Angels)
with the author's reply to his critics. London:
Ernest Benn, 1925.
*Three Plays with a Preface (Home Chat, Sirocco, This
Was a Man).* London: Secker, 1928. In USA, *The
Plays of Noël Coward* (New York: Doubleday,
1928).
Bitter-Sweet, and Other Plays (Easy Virtue, Hay Fever),

with a few comments on the younger dramatists by
W. Somerset Maugham. New York: Doubleday, 1929.

Collected Sketches and Lyrics, with an introduction by Coward.
London: Hutchinson, 1931.

Curtain Calls. New York: Doubleday 1940. *(To-Night at 8.30,
Conversation Piece, Easy Virtue, Point Valaine, This Was a
Man.)*

The Noël Coward Song Book, with an introduction and annotations
by Coward. London: Joseph, 1953.

The Lyrics of Noël Coward, with an introduction by Coward.
London: Heinemann, 1965; Methuen, 1983.

Articles and Essays

'Introduction' to *Contemporary Theatre, 1924* by James Agate
(London: Chapman and Hall, 1925).

'Light Music Seriously' (1: 'In the Days of My Youth'; 2: 'My
Own Contributions'; 3: 'How the Numbers Came'), *Punch,*
8, 15, 22 July 1953.

'I Defend the Star System', *Sunday Express,* 8 Aug., 1954.

'Noël Coward Looks at the Theatre Today' (1: 'These Old-
Fashioned Revolutionaries'; 2: 'The Scratch-and-Mumble
School'; 3: 'A Warning to the Critics'), *Sunday Times,* 15,
22, 29 July 1961.

Interviews

Daily Mail, 13 May 1960, with Cecil Wilson.

Time and Tide, 10-16 Jan. 1963, with Ian Sproat.

Daily Mail, 5 June 1964, with David Lewin.

The Listener, 7 Apr. 1966, with Michael Macowan.

The Times, 26 July 1966, with Stella King.

Sunday Times, 16 Nov. 1969, with John Heilpern

The Listner, 12 Oct. 1966, with Edgar Lusgarten.

Playback, Vol. 1 (London: Davis Poynter, 1973), with Ronald
Hayman.

The Listener, 22 May 1975, as 'The Wit and Wisdom of the
Master'. [Collected from BBC Archives, mainly Coward on
acting with interpolated poems.]

b: Secondary Sources

Full-Length Studies

Patrick Braybrook, *The Amazing Mr. Noël Coward.* London:
Denis Archer, 1933. [Adulatory in tone, this piece is repre-

sentative of the kind of critical approval of Coward which drew O'Casey's fire in his 'Coward Codology' (see below).]

Rose Snider, *Satire in the Comedies of Congreve, Sheridan, Wilde, and Coward*. Oronto, Maine: University of Maine Press, 1933 (University of Maine Studies, Second Series, No. 42).

Robert Graecen, *The Art of Noël Coward*. Aldington, Kent: Hand and Flower Press, 1953. [Argues for Coward's status on the basis of 'serious' plays.]

Dick Richards, ed. *The Wit of Noël Coward*. London: Leslie Frewin, 1968. [*Bon mots,* one-liners, etc, trawled from a variety of written and reported sources.]

Milton Levin, *Noël Coward*. New York: Twayne Publishers, 1968 (Twayne's English Author's Series, No. 73). [Includes useful critical bibliography.]

Sheridan Morley, *A Talent to Amuse*. London: Heinemann, 1969; Harmondsworth: Penguin, 1975. (Critical, well-researched biography, with good bibliography including memoirs of Coward's contemporaries.]

John Hadfield, ed., *Cowardy Custard: the World of Noël Coward,* . . . a series of pictorial commentaries on the theme of some of Coward's lyrics and sketches, based on the production of the same name at the Mermaid Theatre, London, 10 July 1972. London: Samuel French 1900.

Charles Castle, *Noël*. London: W.H.Allen., 1972. [Based on extracts from plays, autobiographies and reminiscences of contemporaries.]

Clarence Ralph Morse, *Mad Dogs and Englishmen: a Study of Noël Coward*. Emporia: Kansas State Teachers College 1973. [Slight.]

William Marchant, *The Privilege of His Company: Noël Coward Remembered*. London: Weidenfeld and Nicholson, 1975; Indianapolis: Bobbs-Merrill, 1975.

Cole Lesley, *The Life of Noël Coward*. London: Cape, 1976; Harmondsworth: Penguin, 1978; as *Remembered Laughter,* New York: Knopf, 1976. [Highly personal account by member of Coward's personal staff for nearly 40 years.]

C.R. Yaravintelimath, *Jesting Jeremiah: a Study of Noël Coward's Comic Vision*. Dharwad: Karnatak University, 1978 (Research Publications series).

Cole Lesley, *Noël Coward and his Friends*. London: Weidenfeld and Nicholson, 1979.

John Lahr, *Coward the Playwright*. London: Methuen, 1982. [Interpretive study of key plays and balanced discussion of critical reception of Coward's work. Good bibliography.]

Articles and Chapters in Books

James Agate, 'The Naughty Playwrights' in *A Short View of the English Stage* (London: Herbert Jenkins, 1927). [On the character-types of Coward, Lonsdale, Arlen, etc.]

A.G. Macdonell, 'The Plays of Mr. Noël Coward', *London Mercury*, Nov. 1931. [Argues that *Post-Mortem* is the strongest indication that Coward may become a 'real dramatist'.]

Alpha and Omega, 'Noël Coward', *Saturday Review,* 8 Jan. 1933. ['For and against'.]

J.C. Furnas, 'The Art of Noël Coward', *Fortnightly Review,* Dec. 1933. [Coward's plays in the context of post-war disillusionment and 'Moral Fascism'.]

George Jean Nathan, 'Noël Coward', in *The Magic Mirror,* ed. Thomas Quinn Curtis (New York: Knopf, 1969). [Reprinted from *Passing Judgements,* 1935: argues that Coward's sophisticated 'wit' is heavily indebted to vaudeville sketches.]

Frank Swinnerton, 'Noël Coward', in *The Georgian Literary Scene 1910-1935* (Hutchinson, 1935).

Sean O'Casey, 'Coward Codology', in *The Flying Wasp* (London: Macmillan, 1937. [Trenchant attack on Coward and his critical supporters.]

J.C. Trewin, 'The Plays of Noël Coward', *Adelphi,* xxvii, No. 4 (1951).

Kenneth Tynan, 'Noël Coward', *Evening Standard*, 4 July 1953; reprinted in *Curtains* (London: Longmans, 1961). [General appreciation of Coward's work, with evocative description of Coward in cabaret.]

Robert Bolt, 'Mr. Coward Had the Last of the Wine', *Sunday Times,* 29 Jan. 1961. [A reply to Coward's attack on 'new wave' theatre in the same newspaper (see above).]

Kenneth Tynan, 'Let Coward Flinch', in *Tynan Right and Left* (London: Longmans, 1967. [Response to Coward's attack on the 'new wave' in *Sunday Times,* 1961.]

John Weightman, 'Theatre: on Not Appreciating Mr. Coward', *Encounter,* 27 July 1966. [Expresses 'bewilderment' at general critical approval of Coward, and of *A Song at Twilight* in particular.]

John Russell Taylor, *The Rise and Fall of the Well-Made Play* (London: Methuen, 1967).

Beverley Nichols, 'Darling Noël', *Daily Telegraph*, 12 Dec. 1969.

Basil Dean, 'Early Coward', in *Seven Stages: an Autobiography 1888-1927.* London, Hutchinson, 1970. in [Dean directed

Easy Virtue, The Queen Was in the Parlour, Home Chat, and *Sirocco.*]

Betka Zamoyska, 'To Darling Noël Who Has Flown away to Sunny Cove', *Nova,* June 1973. [Obituary.]

Harold Hobson, 'Sir Noël Coward: Playwright-Actor who Was Master of Comedy', *The Times,* 27 Mar. 1973. [Obituary.]

W.A. Darlington, 'Noël Coward, Master Craftsman of Theatre', *Daily Telegraph,* 27 Mar. 1973. [Obituary.]

Kenneth Tynan, 'Exit a Man with a Talent to Amuse', *The Observer,* 1 Apr. 1973.

W.A. Darlington, 'The Mastery of Coward', *Daily Telegraph,* 14 Jan. 1974.

Albert Hunt, 'Pinter and Coward', *New Society,* 24 June 1976. [On Pinter's production of *Blithe Spirit.*]

John Fisher, 'Noël Coward', in *Call Them Irreplaceable* (London: Elm Tree Books, 1976). [Tribute to Coward as an all-round entertainer.]

Guido Almansi, 'Writing Like Tickling: on Noël Coward', *Encounter,* May 1977.

David Robinson, 'When Hitchcock Adapted Noël Coward', *The Times,* 25 Apr. 1977. [On film version of *Easy Virtue.*]

John Wells, 'The Master Inside Out', *London Magazine,* Dec. 1977.

John Elsom, *Post-War British Theatre* (London: Routledge, 1976), p. 25-34. [Discusses Coward as prototype English actor].

Douglas Dunn, 'Pity the Poor Philosopher: Coward's Comic Genius', *Encounter,* Oct. 1980. [Plays up to 1941, with a defence of their 'theatricality']

John Lahr, 'The Politics of Charm', *New Society,* 12 Mar. 1981.

Alastair Forbes, 'Memories of the Master', *The Spectator,* 11 Sept. 1982. [Review of Coward's *Diaries.*]

David Hare and Nicholas Shrimpton, 'Noël Coward: For . . . and Against', *Times Literary Supplement,* 1 Oct. 1982.

Reference Sources

Raymond Mander and Joe Mitchenson, *Theatrical Companion to Coward,* with an introduction by Terence Rattigan. London: Rockcliff, 1957. [Comprehensive and authoritative guide to productions, publications, recordings, and films to 1957, with plot summaries of plays. Essential.]

Enoch Brater, 'Noël Coward', in *Dictionary of Literary Biography, Vol. Ten: Modern British Dramatists 1900-1945,* ed. Stanley Weintraub (Detroit: Gale Research, 1982), p. 116-29.